A STAGE 6
NEWBURY HOUSE READER

LIFE, LIBERTY AND THE PURSUIT OF HAPPINESS

Historical Readings

Mary Ann Kearny
James Baker

NEWBURY HOUSE PUBLISHERS, INC.

ROWLEY / MASSACHUSETTS

Library of Congress Cataloging in Publication Data

Kearny, Mary Ann.
    Life, liberty and the pursuit of happiness.

    (Newbury House readers)
    1. English language--Text-books for foreigners.
2. Readers--United States.   I. Baker, James Thomas,
joint author. II. Title.
PE1128.K4   428'.2'4   78-1761
ISBN 0-88377-111-X

NEWBURY HOUSE PUBLISHERS, INC.

Language Science
Language Teaching
Language Learning

ROWLEY, MASSACHUSETTS 01969

Cover art by Barbara Frake.

Printed in the U.S.A.   First printing: March 1978
                                                    5   4   3   2

to
Ned Kearny and Betsy Baker

Contents

Foreword

This book is a child of necessity. In 1976, after our university's foreign student population had grown to considerable size, Dr. James Baker designed a course in American history specifically for these students. He could find no textbook which was appropriate and decided that one should be written. The book that has emerged represents the combined efforts of two teachers in different disciplines—Baker in history and Mary Ann Kearny in English as a Second Language.

The text is based on a series of historical essays written by James Baker. It is intended to give a broad, interpretive introduction to the American historical experience. At the same time, it is a textbook designed to teach English language skills. The Introduction offers explanations and instructions for using the book in English as a Second Language (ESL) classrooms.

We wish to acknowledge the help of many colleagues—above all, Professors Edward Kearny of the Department of Government and Richard Troutman of the Department of History at Western Kentucky University. They provided invaluable professional suggestions throughout the preparation of this book. We would also like to express our appreciation to Dr. Jack McGregor for his help on the first chapter and to Dr. Ron Eckard, Donna Bunch, and John Heins who used the manuscript in their ESL classes and made many useful suggestions. Many thanks go to our ever-patient typist, Ikey Lucas, and others who also worked on the manuscript. Finally, there is a personal word of thanks to Rupert Ingram and Jo Alexander, at Newbury House, for their very special encouragement.

Mary Ann Kearny

James Baker

Western Kentucky University
1978

Introduction
Information for Teachers

Life, Liberty and the Pursuit of Happiness is written within the vocabulary controls of Stage 6 of the Newbury House graded reader series. It is designed for use by university students, high school students or others who wish to learn more about the history and culture of the United States and to improve their English language skills. Although the vocabulary is controlled, the ideas are often complex and will appeal to the mature reader. For each chapter, *Questions for Discussion and Composition* contains a number of questions about the students' native countries. Teachers will probably wish to have students discuss and write about aspects of the history and culture of their countries.

It is important to work with the chapters in the order in which they are presented. Ideas which are introduced in the first chapter are developed or mentioned in later chapters. Also, the *vocabulary is cumulative.* That is, new vocabulary words introduced in the first chapters are repeated in the text and exercises of succeeding chapters. An alphabetical listing of new words introduced in the text, and not explained in a footnote, follows each chapter.

This material is appropriate for students who have a "high intermediate" or "low advanced" proficiency in English as a Second Language. The average ESL class often contains students with varying degrees of language proficiency, especially at the intermediate level. The teacher may wish to vary assignments according to the levels of students' proficiency. For this reason, it is suggested that the teacher first skim the exercise material at the end of each chapter before making specific assignments. There are a number of ways to use this material and each chapter contains several types of exercises.

The exercises are divided into two sections. Exercises in Section One can probably be completed in an hour of class time. These exercises check students' comprehension of the ideas, the words, and the phrases of the chapter, and provide opportunities for expanding vocabulary through exercises on word forms, synonyms and antonyms, and sentence construction. There are also several exercises on articles, punctuation, and prepositions and verb completers throughout the book.

For each chapter there is a cloze exercise which is a paragraph summarizing the chapter. Every fifth word has been deleted and students should fill in the blanks with any word which makes sense. New words and phrases introduced in the chapter may appear in this cloze exercise, requiring students to recall the new words. The teacher should explain what a summary is, and should point out that this cloze exercise paragraph summarizes the chapter. It should also be pointed out that summary paragraphs are often found in textbooks written in English on various subjects.

Section Two contains additional exercises which may be used to supplement Section One, but it is primarily concerned with the organization of ideas—for reading and for writing.

ESL teachers often use reading selections as the stimulus for composition writing, since reading provides not only ideas but also vocabulary and structures useful for writing. In turn, writing reinforces the learning of new vocabulary and structures, as students use them to communicate in English.

The ability to organize information is a skill which is part of both good reading and good writing. The educational system of the United States, and probably most of Western Europe, teaches students to process and organize information in a particular way: in terms of main ideas and supporting details. Students are taught to read for main ideas, distinguishing them from more detailed information. When writing, they are expected first to present their main ideas clearly, and then to support them with the necessary details. Often, this information is arranged in outline form at some time during the process.

Outlining is a skill which is taught to American students, and it is a fundamental part of the American system of education. Although American educators may not use the formalities of

Roman numerals and capital letters, they generally think, lecture, and write in outline form. A professor whose lecture does not follow some kind of an outline is said to be disorganized.

For students who come from other countries to study in the United States, outlining is a very useful skill. It helps them understand how Americans think and write, and shows them what will be expected of them in their studies—taking lecture notes, reading textbooks, answering essay examination questions, and writing research papers.

For these reasons, there are outlines and outlining exercises for each chapter in this book. The first chapter has a step-by-step presentation of the organization of the material in the chapter, leading to the chapter outline. It explains what an outline is and then asks students to make a simple outline and write a paragraph following the outline. It would be wise for the teacher to read the explanation of the organization of the chapter aloud to the class, guiding the students as they identify the various sections of the chapter. The teacher can then point out how the chapter outline summarizes the information in each section.

In classes which are using the outlining exercises in Section Two, the teacher should have students read the outline before they read the chapter, in order to help them anticipate information they will read. Using the outline to preview the chapter will encourage students to read for ideas. The teacher may also use the chapter outline for reference while discussing the main ideas of the chapter after the students have read it. The chapter outline can also be used to teach skimming by asking students to skim for specific information presented in the outline.

The outlining exercises become more difficult toward the end of the book. The goal is to have students eventually write their own outlines for their own compositions. More advanced students will be capable of doing this from the beginning. As soon as the procedure for making outlines has been established, these advanced students should be assigned composition topics and asked to write their own outlines and compositions. The *Questions for Discussion and Composition* exercises may be used for this purpose.

Students who are less advanced should not be given such freedom; those who have difficulty at the sentence level should not be asked to write full compositions. Instead, these students should be assigned paragraphs to write. There are some exercises on writing paragraphs in this text, but the teacher will probably want to supplement these exercises with other writing activities.

A teacher must be flexible and adapt texts to the needs of real-life students. I have had many real-life students with many different needs, and many of the activities in this book are the product of an ongoing effort to meet these needs. Whatever teaching situation you have, I hope this text will be helpful. Most of all, I hope it will be fun.

Mary Ann Kearny

Life, Liberty
and the
Pursuit of Happiness

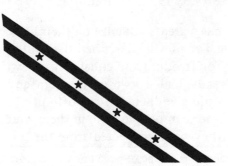

CHAPTER 1
THE AMERICAN LAND

This land is your land—this land is my land.
From California—to the New York Island.
From the redwood[1] forests—to the Gulf Stream's waters.
This land was made for you and me.
                              —Woody Guthrie (folk singer) 1963

The land where people live has a great influence on their lives. In the early 1830s, Alexis de Tocqueville described the United States as an excellent place for freedom and equality to grow. He said that the people already had a love of freedom and equality, but that the land would give them the opportunity to remain free and equal. The American people were in the center of a large continent, where they were protected from the rest

[1]*redwood*: The redwood, or Sequoia, is a type of large tree which grows on the west coast of America.

A land of great variety

of the world. De Tocqueville wrote in 1832, "The Americans have no neighbors, and consequently they have no great wars." There was no need, then, to have great armies. The people were able to spend their time and energy and their money developing their land.

There was plenty of land to develop. The continent was large, and there was plenty of land for everyone who came. The land was also very rich; there were great natural resources. There were great forests and rivers which gave them wood and water power. There was much fertile farmland. The opportunities and the natural resources seemed endless. The land was not controlled by a small group of wealthy people, as it was in Europe. Large numbers of people had an opportunity to own land. In these ways, the land strengthened the Americans' idea of freedom and equality.

The size of the land has had an effect on the history of the United States. At first, most people lived on the Atlantic coast because the Appalachian Mountains stopped them from moving westward. These mountains run from north to south in the eastern part of the United States. They are not very high mountains—often less than 3,000 feet—but they are close together. Daniel Boone found a way to pass through the mountains, and, by the late 1700s, people began to follow him westward.

On the other side of the Appalachian Mountains the people found the north-central plains. For three million years, ice had brought rich land down from Canada and made these plains. The land is unusually fertile and is therefore excellent for farming. More and more people came to settle this new land. Then, in the early 1800s, the settlers crossed the great Mississippi River. The Mississippi runs from north to south, and empties into the Gulf of Mexico. In some places it is a mile wide. Including the Ohio and the Missouri Rivers, which empty into it at the center of the country, the Mississippi River is the longest river in the world.

On the other side of the Mississippi River, the fertile north-central plains continue for several hundred miles. Then there is more flat land which is not so fertile, called the Great Plains. These plains run from north to south, covering a half a million square miles. The land is often dry and very few trees grow there. For many years people thought it was a desert, and few settlers chose to live there.

In the western part of the United States there are high mountains, called the Rocky Mountains (the Rockies), which run from north to south, covering nearly one-third of the United States. They are much higher than the Appalachians in the East: some of them are 12,000 to 14,000 feet high. On the other side of the Rockies is the Pacific coast. Until 1849, there were only a few settlers on the Pacific coast; in that year, gold was discovered in California, and large numbers of people hurried to the west coast.

Today, the United States stretches across the North American continent from the Atlantic Ocean to the Pacific

Ocean. It is about 2,700 miles (4,800 kilometers) from its east coast to its west coast. From its northern border with Canada to its southern border with Mexico, it is about 1,400 miles (3,200 kilometers). It is possible to go halfway across the northern United States by water. Ships can travel from the Atlantic Ocean, down the St. Lawrence River and Seaway, into the five Great Lakes, which form the eastern half of the border with Canada. Water borders the southern states also. The Gulf of Mexico forms half of the southern border of the United States.

Forty-eight of the fifty states are within these borders: two are not. These are the two newest states—Alaska and Hawaii—which became states in 1959. Alaska is located on the northwestern border of Canada. The United States bought it from Russia in 1867. At that time, a number of people criticized the government for buying it, saying that it was a cold, empty place, but now Alaska is considered an important state. Located only a few miles from the Russian border, Alaska has important natural resources—gold, wood, and oil. Alaskan oil has become very important to the United States. The Alaskan pipeline, which was completed in 1977, pipes Alaskan oil across the state to the ocean where ships are loaded to take the oil to American oil refineries.[2]

The state of Hawaii is quite different. It is a group of eight islands in the middle of the Pacific Ocean. The weather is warm and sunny all year long, and this pleasant climate makes Hawaii a popular state. People from all over the world have come to live there—Japanese, Chinese, Koreans, Filipinos, Puerto Ricans, Europeans, and people from the mainland[3] United States—and the state is also visited by many tourists who come to enjoy the climate, and the natural beauty of the islands.

All fifty states are different in many ways. In discussing the United States, one can speak of northern states and southern states, but most Americans also describe their country another

---

[2]*an oil refinery*: A factory where oil is cleaned and prepared for sale.
[3]*mainland*: continental

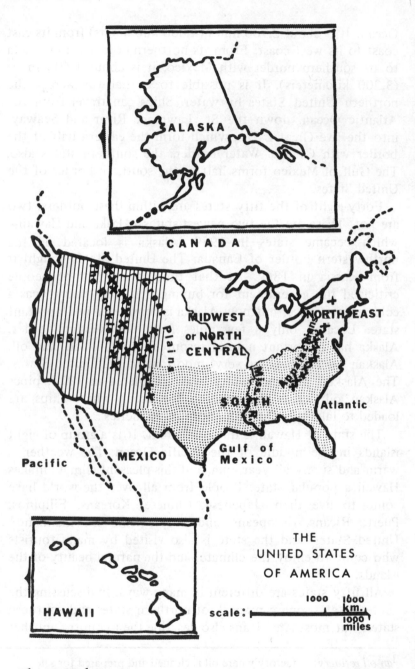

The United States

Kearny and Baker

way, by dividing it into four regions—the Northeast, the South, the Midwest, and the West. The map on page 6 shows these regions.

The Northeast: The Northeast is the oldest region in the United States, except for Virginia, a southern state which was settled in 1607. The settlement of the Northeast began in 1620, in Massachusetts.

The great cities of the Northeast are Boston, Philadelphia, and New York City. They are famous partly because so many important events in American history occurred there, and because they lead the nation today in so many areas, such as business, banking, education, fashion, music, theater, etc.

Washington, located in the District of Columbia, is also considered a northeastern city. Washington, D.C., is the capital of the United States, and the center of government and political life.

The Northeast is a highly industrialized region, with great factories and crowded cities. The Northeast is where American industry began, but it is more than an industrial center. In some parts of the Northeast there are small fishing towns and miles of fertile and beautiful farmland. Several of the New England states have no big cities at all.

The South: The South is a region which is experiencing considerable change, so that Americans sometimes speak of the "Old South" and the "New South." The Old South had large farms, little industry, and few large cities. The population was small, and the people had a strong feeling of "regionalism"; that is, they loved their region—the South. This was partly because of the Civil War (1861-1865). During the Civil War, the southerners fought for four years to make the South a separate nation.

The North won the Civil War and the South remained part of the United States. The South continued to be different from the North in many ways for nearly a hundred years. Since the 1960s, however, there has been great change. Industry has grown in the South. Large cities have developed—New Orleans, Atlanta, Miami, Birmingham. People from all over the country have moved into the South. In 1977,

Jimmy Carter became President. He is one of the few modern American Presidents who have come from the South. Carter has spoken of the change from the Old South to the New South. He said he could not have been elected President if this change had not occurred.

The Midwest: The Midwest is sometimes called the "breadbasket" of the United States, since most of the wheat used to make bread is grown in this region. The Midwest produces more farm products than any other region in the world, and much of the food Americans eat comes from the Midwest. Wheat and corn are grown there; cattle and pigs are raised[4] there.

The Midwest includes the fertile farmland of the north-central plains, but it is also an important industrial area. Detroit is the center of the car industry. There are a number of other industrial cities near the Great Lakes. The largest and most famous of these cities is Chicago, with a population of almost 7 million. There are many industries in Chicago. One of them is called "meat-packing." The meat-packing industry prepares meat for sale in stores. Large numbers of cattle and pigs are brought to meat-packing centers where they are killed, and the meat is cut up and prepared for sale.

The West: The West was the last region to be settled. There were few settlers on the Great Plains until the 1860s. In 1862 the government began giving the land away—free. It gave 160 acres[5] to settlers who would live on the land for at least five years. The stories of the settling of the West are popular around the world. Many movies have been made about cowboys and life in the West, and the movie industry itself is in the West, in California.

California has the largest population of any state in the country: one out of every ten Americans lives in the state of California. Over three million people live in San Francisco, while seven million live in and around the city of Los Angeles.

---

[4]*to raise an animal*: To keep and feed it in order to use it for food, clothing, etc.

[5]*an acre*: A measurement of land area, 4,840 square yards.

Los Angeles covers a larger area than any other city in the United States, over 460 square miles.

The West is a region of great variety. Although the Pacific Northwest area is cool and rainy, much of the West is hot and dry, and there are large desert areas. The Southwest gets less than 10 inches of rain a year. Finding water has always been a problem there. In many areas, water must be piped into fields where crops are grown. Many fruits and vegetables are grown in this way.

The West is an area of great natural beauty. The highest mountain in the continental U.S. is there—Mount Whitney. The lowest place is there, too—Death Valley. There are still large, unsettled areas. Many westerners would like to protect these areas. They want the land to remain unsettled; they like the open spaces.

The large, open spaces are disappearing in many regions of the United States. Most Americans now live in cities and towns. Over seventy-three percent live in urban areas of 50,000 people or more. Urban areas now cover over fourteen percent of the land, and it is sometimes hard to see where one city stops and the next one begins. The area around New York City is like this. There seems to be one continuous city from Washington, D.C., to Baltimore, Philadelphia, New York, and on to Boston. Together, the cities spread over 600 square miles. In 1970 there were 49 million people living in this one large urban area.

Americans from all regions love their land. They spend a lot of time outdoors.[6] Camping has become very popular. There are 37 large national parks in the United States. In 1977, Americans made 280 million visits to these parks and found many of them crowded. So many people were camping that there was not enough space for everyone.

Not having enough space is a new problem for Americans. The United States is a very large land and, until recently, Americans believed there would always be plenty of land. If one area became crowded or polluted, they moved to another.

---

[6]*outdoors*: outside

They did not make plans for the land, and they wasted many of its natural resources. Now, much of the good land has been covered with factories and cities, and pollution is a terrible problem.

Today, many Americans believe they must begin to protect their land. They will need better laws to stop pollution. They will need to plan for open spaces. If they want to continue to enjoy their land, they must be more careful to protect it in the future.

NEW WORDS

to be located   To be in a place.
a resource   A material which can be used (oil, wood, etc.).
westward   Toward the west.

EXERCISES

Section One

A. Circle the letter next to the best answer.

1. In 1832 De Tocqueville said that the Americans did not have great wars because
   a. there were no powerful countries near them.
   b. they did not have an army.
   c. they loved peace and did not want war.

2. In the 1830s, large numbers of people in the United States
   a. had no opportunity to own land because it was controlled by a small group of wealthy people.
   b. had no opportunity to own land because it was rich in natural resources and therefore expensive to buy.
   c. had an opportunity to own land because it was not controlled by a small group of wealthy people.

3. In the earliest years of America's history, most of the people
   a. lived on the Pacific coast.
   b. lived on the Atlantic coast.
   c. lived on the Great Plains.

4. The north-central plains area
   a. does not have good farmland.
   b. was settled in the 1600s.
   c. has rich, fertile farmland.

5. All of the states except Hawaii
   a. are on the North American continent.
   b. have borders with other states.
   c. are south of the Canadian border.

6. Today, the Northeast
   a. is one continuous city.
   b. still has some areas of farmland.
   c. is not an industrial area.

7. Most of the U.S. farm products come from
   a. the Midwest.
   b. the West.
   c. the South.

8. Today, the city which covers the biggest area of land is
   a. New York City.
   b. Los Angeles.
   c. San Francisco.

9. The author *implies but does not actually say* that in the early 1800s
   a. the United States needed to develop a large army to protect itself from other countries.
   b. if it had been necessary to have a large army, the people would not have had the time and money to settle the land.
   c. if a nation has an army, it will have to fight great wars.

10. The author *implies but does not actually say* that in the early 1800s
    a. there was a small group of wealthy people who controlled the land in the United States.
    b. the opportunity to own land gave people freedom from certain controls.
    c. there was not enough land for everyone who wanted it.

B. Circle the letter next to the best answer.

1. There were great natural *resources*.
   a. beautiful areas
   b. national parks
   c. materials which can be used

2. The size of the land has had an effect on the *history* of the United States.
   a. what happened in the past
   b. all of the parts of the land
   c. in all areas of life

3. For three million years, ice had brought rich land down from Canada and made these *plains*.
   a. farmland
   b. flat land
   c. valleys

4. More and more people came to *settle* this new land.
   a. They came to live there.
   b. They discovered the land.
   c. They explored the land.

5. Alaska is located off the northwestern *border* of Canada.
   a. coast
   b. shore
   c. the land where two neighboring countries meet

6. The Northeast is a highly industrialized *region*.
   a. city
   b. factories
   c. part of the country

7. *Urban areas* now cover over 14% of the land.
   a. farms
   b. cities
   c. unsettled areas

8. *Pollution* is a terrible problem.
   a. wasting the land
   b. crowded cities
   c. dirty air and water

9. De Toqueville wrote in 1832, "The Americans have no neighbors, and *consequently* they have no great wars."
   a. therefore
   b. because
   c. also

10. A number of people *criticized* the government for buying Alaska.
    a. They said it was a good idea.
    b. They said it was a bad idea.
    c. They thanked the government for buying it.

C. Choose the word form which correctly completes each sentence. Put verbs into the correct tense. If necessary, make nouns plural.

Example: continent, continental
   a. The seven *continents* of the world are Africa, Antarctica, Asia, Australia, Europe, North America and South America.
   b. When people speak of the *continental* U.S., they usually mean the 48 states whose borders touch each other.

1. history, historian, historical, historically
   a. A . . . . . . is a person who studies things that happened in the past.
   b. In the New England states, there are many places of . . . . . . interest and importance.
   c. The size of the land has had an effect on the . . . . . . of the United States.
   d. . . . . . ., the Northeast has been a center of power and influence.

2. settler, settlement, to settle, settled
   a. Many people decided . . . . . . in the Midwest because the land was excellent for farming.
   b. Few . . . . . . chose to live in the Great Plains area.
   c. The . . . . . . of the Northeast began in the 1600s.
   d. In the late 1700s, people began leaving the . . . . . . areas of the Northeast to move westward.

3. region, regionalism, regional
   a. There are some . . . . . . differences in the way Americans speak.

　　b. The speech of people from the southern . . . . . . of the United States sounds quite different from that of the people from the North.

　　c. The South is an area where there has been a strong feeling of . . . .

4. urbanization, urban, urbanized

　　a. An . . . . . . area is one where the population is more than 50,000.

　　b. As a country becomes more industrialized, it also becomes more . . . .

　　c. . . . . . . has brought problems such as crowding, more crime and pollution.

5. pollution, to pollute, polluted

　　a. Industry has done much . . . . . . both the air and water.

　　b. In large cities such as Los Angeles, the air . . . . . . is especially bad.

　　c. In some regions, people are trying to clean up the . . . . . . lakes and rivers.

6. location, to be located

　　a. Many important cities of the United States . . . . . . along rivers or near lakes.

　　b. The . . . . . . of a city has a certain influence on its development.

7. variety, to vary, various

　　a. The climate . . . . . . greatly in the United States.

　　b. The states differ from each other in a . . . . . . of ways.

　　c. In the . . . . . . regions of the U.S., one can find some areas which are hot and dry and others which are cool and rainy.

8. industry, industrialization, industrialize, industrial

　　a. Since World War II, southerners have tried to . . . . . . their region.

　　b. . . . . . . has brought a number of new . . . . . . to the South.

　　c. One of the greatest . . . . . . areas of the United States goes from Pittsburg, Pennsylvania to Chicago, Illinois.

9. criticism, to criticize, critical, critically

　　a. In 1867, a number of people . . . . . . the government for buying Alaska.

　　b. The people who were . . . . . . of the decision did not know that there were valuable natural resources there.

c. They spoke . . . . . . of Alaska as a cold, empty place.
d. If people had known there was gold in Alaska, there probably would have been no . . . . . . of the decision to buy it.

10. equality, to equal, equal, equally
    a. De Toqueville said that the land of the United States gave the people the opportunity to remain free and . . . .
    b. The land strengthened their idea of . . . .
    c. Large numbers of people shared . . . . . . in the development of the land.
    d. Plenty of land plus great natural resources . . . . . . a land of opportunity.

D. Use each group of words to make a sentence. Add other words, but use the words below in the form and order they are given.

Example: people, had, love, freedom, equality.
   The people had a love of freedom and equality.

1. more, more, people, came, settle, land
2. north-central plains, excellent, farming
3. other side, Rockies, is, Pacific coast
4. 1849, gold, discovered, California
5. climate, continental United States, varied
6. Northeast, oldest region, United States
7. settlement, Northeast, began, 1620, Massachusetts
8. Detroit, center, car industry
9. West, last region, settled
10. one, ten Americans, lives, state, California

E. The following paragraph is a summary of the chapter. Fill in the blanks with any word that makes sense.

The American land has _____ the people many opportunities. _____ was plenty of good _____ for the people who _____ to settle in America. _____ settlements began on the _____ coast. The settlers crossed _____ Appalachian Mountains and found _____ plains. Across the Mississippi _____ there are the Great _____ and the high Rocky _____ . Today, the United States _____ from the Atlantic Ocean _____ the Pacific Ocean. The _____ States borders Canada to _____ north and Mexico to _____ south. All fifty states _____ within these borders except _____ and Hawaii. There are _____ great regions—the Northeast,

_____South, the Midwest and _____ West. In many regions _____the country, the large _____ spaces are disappearing. There _____ many cities covering the_____. Pollution is a problem. _____ will have to protect_____land in the future.

F. *Questions for Discussion and Composition.*

1. How has the size of the land influenced the development of the United States? Why did so many people have an opportunity to own land? What effect has this had on Americans?

2. Describe the size of your country. How has the size of your country influenced its development? What natural resources are there in your country? How many people own and control the land? What effect does this have on your country?

3. De Tocqueville said that the United States was protected from the rest of the world. It did not have to fight great wars in order to gain new land. What effect do neighboring countries have on a nation's development? What are the advantages of having powerful neighboring countries? What are the disadvantages?

4. Describe the borders of your country. Have the borders changed in the last one hundred years? What countries share a border with your country? Do the borders of your country touch an ocean? How does having an ocean border affect a country?

5. Describe the regions of your country. What is the climate like? Is it varied? Is there a good supply of water in all parts of your country? How do the climate and the water supply of a country affect its development? Is there a feeling of regionalism in your country?

6. Describe the great cities of your country. Where are they located? Are there large urban areas? Are there large unsettled areas? What plans has your government made for using the land? How much of a problem is pollution?

Section Two

A. Fill in the blanks with *the, a* or *an,* as needed. If no article is needed, write an *X* in the blank.

   Example: __X__ Alaska and __X__ Hawaii are _the_ two newest states.

_____ Alaska is located on _____ northwestern border of _____ Canada. _____ United States bought it from _____ Russia in _____ 1867. At that time, _____ number of people criticized _____ government for buying it, saying that it was _____ cold, empty place, but now, _____ Alaska is considered _____ important state. Located only _____ few miles from _____ Russian border, it has _____ important natural resources— _____ gold, _____ wood, and _____ oil. _____ Alaskan oil has become very important to _____ United States. _____ Alaskan pipeline, which was completed in _____ 1977, pipes _____ Alaskan oil across _____ state to _____ ocean, where _____ ships are loaded to take _____ oil to _____ American oil refineries.

B. Write capital letters, commas, periods and parentheses where they are needed.

today the united states stretches across the north american continent from the atlantic ocean to the pacific ocean it is about 2700 miles 4800 kilometers from its east coast to its west coast from its northern border with canada to its southern border with mexico it is about 1400 miles 3200 kilometers it is possible to go halfway across the northern united states by water ships can travel from the atlantic ocean down the st lawrence river and seaway into the five great lakes which form the eastern half of the border with canada water borders the southern states also the gulf of mexico forms half of the southern border of the united states

C. Suppose you were asked to give a short speech[1] about your country. How would you describe the land? You would probably want to include some of this information:

1. the location
2. the borders
3. the geographical features (the important rivers, lakes, mountains, plains, deserts, etc.)
4. the climate
5. the important cities
6. the natural resources

---

[1] *to give a speech*: To speak to a group of people.

There are many ways to organize such information. This chapter describes the American land, and the author has arranged the information in five parts:

1. the introduction
2. the geographical areas
3. the borders
4. the four regions
5. the conclusion

Reread the chapter very quickly, looking for these five parts. This kind of fast reading is called *skimming*. When you skim, you do not read every word. Instead, you read for ideas.

D. The author has used a plan, called an *outline,* to arrange the information about the American land. An outline is a list of ideas. It lists the main ideas and the details which support or develop these ideas. By skimming, you have found the five parts of this chapter: these are the main ideas. The outline below lists these main ideas with Roman numerals[2] (I, II, III, etc.). The details which support or develop the main ideas are listed under them (A, B, C, etc.), and further details are listed under 1, 2, 3, etc.

Chapter Outline: The American Land

I. The introduction: the importance of the great size of the land
   A. Protection from great foreign powers
   B. Opportunities for many people to own good land

II. The geographical areas
   A. The Atlantic coast
   B. The Appalachian Mountains
   C. The fertile, north-central plains
   D. The Mississippi River
   E. The Great Plains
   F. The Rocky Mountains
   G. The Pacific coast

---

[2]*a numeral*: a number

III. The borders
    A. Eastern
    B. Western
    C. Northern
    D. Southern
    E. States outside these borders
       1. Alaska
       2. Hawaii

IV. The regions
    A. The Northeast
    B. The South
    C. The Midwest
    D. The West

V. The conclusion
    A. The growth of cities
    B. The wasting of land
       1. Crowding
       2. Pollution
    C. The need to protect the land for the future

E. Write an outline of the regions of your country, using the outline below.

    I. The regions of my country
       A. _____
       B. _____
       C. _____

F. Write a paragraph about the regions of your country, following the outline you have written in Exercise E.

A nation of immigrants

Kearny and Baker

CHAPTER 2
THE PEOPLE

America, thou[1] half-brother of the world;
With something good and bad of every land.
— Philip Bailey (poet) 1816-1902

The United States of America is a young country. It is only 200 years old. Its people have come from every region of the world: from Europe, from Africa, and from Asia. One American historian has called America "a nation of immigrants." President John F. Kennedy who was himself the grandson of an Irish immigrant once said that all Americans have in common[2] the fact that sometime in the past "we all got off a boat."[3] The history of the United States is filled with stories of immigrants and the new life they found in America.

Early Immigrants and the British Influence: People began coming to live in North America in the 1600s to find freedom and a better life. Many of them lived together in groups called colonies. There were colonies established by England (Great

---

[1]*thou*: you

[2]*to have in common*: to share

[3]*we all got off a boat*: We—or our ancestors—were immigrants.

Britain), Spain, France, Holland, and Sweden, and large numbers of German immigrants also came. The largest number of colonies was established by the British, and, although immigrants have come to America from many nations, more of them have come from Great Britain (including Scotland and Ireland) than from anywhere else. It was the British who most influenced the early history of the new nation.

The British established colonies along the east coast of North America for several reasons. The first permanent colony was established in Jamestown, Virginia, in 1607, and it and some other colonies were established as centers of trade. The North American continent was rich in natural resources. Britain had factories which needed raw materials, and therefore wanted a permanent trade arrangement with America. Raw materials such as sugar, rice, cotton and tobacco would be sent from the colonies to Britain, and would be used to make products such as glass, clothing and paper in British factories. These finished products would be sent back to the colonies. The trading of raw materials and finished products became important to both the British and the Americans, and trade was an important tie between the two countries for over a hundred years.

There was another reason why the British came to America. Some of them came to find religious freedom. Colonies such as Massachusetts and Pennsylvania were established as homes for certain religious groups, who were having trouble in England because of their beliefs.

One of these groups, the Puritans, established the colony of Massachusetts. They believed that God had led them to America to build a religious nation. Their religious beliefs helped them when life was difficult in the new land. The strong religious beliefs of the Puritans are part of the American heritage. So is the Puritans' belief in hard work. Americans often speak of their "Puritan heritage," which tells them it is important to work hard and have a strong belief in God.

The British have influenced American life in many areas, as well as in the area of religion. They gave the Americans their language, English, and having the same language has been a strong tie between the two nations. Even today, there are few differences between British English and American English. The two groups may sound different when they speak, but they are able to understand each other easily. The written language is almost the same, although there are a few differences in spelling.

There are other areas of life which have been influenced by the British. In 1776, when the Americans decided to establish a new nation separate from England, they kept many British institutions and customs, and the institutions of government and the laws are still very similar. Britain also influenced American culture—the art, music and ideas of the United States. American culture in general is more closely related to that of Britain than to the culture of any other nation, but there have been other important influences also.

American Indians: When the colonists arrived in North America they did not find an empty land. There were people already living in the area—the Native American Indians. Christopher Columbus, who discovered America, named them "Indians." He believed that he had gone all the way around the world and had reached India. In fact, these people probably came to America from Asia at least five thousand years ago. They may have crossed a land or ice bridge from Siberia (Russia) to North America. Large numbers of them settled in Central and South America, and established civilizations there, while a much smaller number settled in North America.

The North American Indians were divided into many groups called "tribes." Each tribe was like a small separate nation, with its own language and its own leaders. The Indians were not strong enough to prevent Europeans from settling in North America. When colonies were established on the east coast, the Indians began moving westward. Many of the Indians had moved west of the Appalachian Mountains by 1776. In the late 1700s and early 1800s, immigrants began coming to the new land in large numbers. The white settlers moved westward, taking Indian land as they went. The Indians were pushed farther and farther west. Some of the Indian tribes fought against the immigrants. But the immigrants had the advantage—they had guns and they had large numbers of soldiers.

By the end of the 1800s, the Indians had been defeated. Areas of land called reservations were given to the Indians, and they were forced to live on them. The story of what happened to those Native Americans is not a happy one. Today, there are between 800,000 and 1,000,000 American Indians in the United States. They no longer have to live on reservations, but about half of them still do. Many of them are very poor, and forty percent of them have no jobs. In recent years people have shown new interest in the American Indians, their culture and their problems. Some Indians have asked the United States government to return land which was taken from their ancestors. Little progress has been made, however. Even today, very few Indians are able to take an active role in American life.

Afro-Americans: Another group of Americans which had an important influence on American culture is the black Afro-Americans. Many Africans were brought to America and sold as slaves from 1619 to 1807. They were not freed until the end of the Civil War in 1865. Most of them worked on large farms in the South. After they were freed, many of the black Americans continued to live in the South. In 1900, ninety percent of them were still living in the South, and many of them worked for the same white people who had owned them or their ancestors before the Civil War. After 1900 they began to leave the South, and, by 1960, fifty percent of the Blacks had moved into the North and West, taking with them their special music, art, and religion. In recent years they have taken a more active role in American life than their ancestors. They are now twelve percent of the American population.

The Civil War (1861-1865) brought many changes in American life. The slaves were freed. Industry began to grow and more people were needed to work in the new factories.

Later Immigrants: New immigrants came in very large numbers, and the population grew quickly. This growth is shown below:

Year	Number of Americans
1800	5,000,000
1850	23,000,000
1900	76,000,000
1950	150,000,000
1970	204,000,000

In the fifty years from 1850 to 1900, the population tripled.[4] These new immigrants were mostly from Europe, but most of them were from Italy and Poland and other countries in southern and eastern Europe. They came to the United States in search of freedom and a better life.

These new immigrants caused many changes in American society. Many of them settled in the eastern industrial cities, bringing their customs and their religion with them. Most of them were Roman Catholics.[5] Almost all the British settlers had been Protestants with similar religious beliefs, and there had been very few Catholics in America until these new immigrants arrived. Today, twenty-five percent of all Americans are Catholic. Furthermore, a number of these new immigrants were Jewish, and today Jews are five percent of the population. After 1900 America could no longer be considered "New" England.

At the same time that these Europeans were coming in large numbers into the eastern urban areas, Asians were coming to the west coast. The largest group was Chinese; the second largest group was Japanese. Some of them came to work on farms, while others came to help build the new railroad across the country. Many of them remained and became successful in business. Their first years in America were often difficult ones, but these people were especially careful with their money, and

---

[4]*tripled*: grew to three times its size

[5]*Protestants and Roman Catholics*: Two separate groups of the Christian religion.

they planned wisely for the future. They also had especially close family ties, and the members of a family helped one another during hard times.

The most recent large group of immigrants is the Latin Americans. Most of them have come from Mexico, Puerto Rico, and Cuba. The Mexicans have settled mostly in California, Texas, and in areas of the Southwest. The Puerto Ricans have settled in New York City, and the Cubans in Florida. These people have brought a new language, Spanish, and a new culture to the United States.

The mixing of so many people from different nations has sometimes caused trouble in America. The Blacks have not been accepted into white society until recently. At times there have been anti-Catholic and anti-Jewish groups. At times when many immigrants arrived at once, American workers have been afraid there would not be enough jobs for everyone. At times there have been efforts to limit immigration, and today there are many laws limiting the number of immigrants.

Eventually, however, the new people have been accepted, and most immigrants have taken an active role in American life. Each nationality has brought America something new, something special. For a long time many people believed that these different nationalities would eventually mix together completely. The playwright[6] Israel Zanwill said that America would become a great "melting pot." All the different nationalities would melt together to form a new race. The old races of the world would form one new "American" race. But so far, this has not happened, and there are still racial and cultural differences.

On all American coins there are the words *E Pluribus Unum*. These Latin words mean "out of many—one." When the United States was established, this was chosen as a motto.[7] America has not proved to be the great melting pot which some people expected. Still, it remains true that out of many races and nationalities has come one nation.

---

[6]*a playwright*: A person who writes plays.

[7]*a motto*: An idea to guide a group or nation.

NEW WORDS

an ancestor   A person in a family who lived long ago.

a heritage   Something which comes to us from the past, from our ancestors.

native   The original people; the people who are born in a country.

a race   People of the same kind or color.

a reservation   Special land kept separate.

to take an active role in   To be very active in; to play an important part in.

a tie   A link.

EXERCISES

Section One

A. Circle the letter next to the best answer.

1. The nation which most influenced the early history of America was
    a. France.
    b. England.
    c. Spain.

2. In the trade arrangement between Britain and her American colonies
    a. finished products such as clothing and glass were sent from America to Britain.
    b. raw materials such as sugar and cotton were sent from America to Britain.
    c. raw materials such as sugar and cotton were sent from Britain to America.

3. The Puritans were
    a. a group of traders.
    b. a religious group.
    c. the native Americans.

4. Christopher Columbus named the Native Americans "Indians" because
    a. they had originally come from India 5,000 years ago.
    b. he brought them to America as slaves.
    c. he thought he had sailed to India.

5. As the white settlers moved westward
   a. they took land from the Indians.
   b. the Indians moved eastward.
   c. the life of the Indians was not changed.

6. The Afro-Americans came to America
   a. as slaves.
   b. to find a better life.
   c. to find religious freedom.

7. After the Civil War, in the late 1800s,
   a. very few immigrants came to the United States.
   b. many more immigrants came.
   c. the number of immigrants remained about the same.

8. Many of the immmigrants who came from southern and eastern Europe
   a. were Protestant.
   b. were Puritans.
   c. were Catholic or Jewish.

9. The author *implies but does not actually say* that
   a. Blacks have not been accepted into white society until recently.
   b. Americans have not always completely accepted people who have a different religion.
   c. there have never been efforts to limit immigration.

10. The author *implies but does not actually say* that
    a. the Indians wanted to live on the reservations.
    b. the Indians would have been happier if they had not been forced to live on the reservations.
    c. the Indians were happy on the reservations.

B. Circle the letter next to the best answer.
   1. Colonies were *established* in America by England, Spain, and France.
      a. taken away
      b. finished
      c. started

   2. The British wanted a *permanent* trade arrangement with the Americans.
      a. They wanted to continue trading with them into the distant future.

b. They wanted to trade with them for a short time.

c. They wanted to earn much money from their trade.

3. *Raw materials* would be sent from the colonies to Britain.
   a. The colonists made things in factories and sent them to Britain.
   b. The colonists did not know how to cook raw food.
   c. The colonists grew crops such as sugar, rice, and cotton and sent them to Britain.

4. In exchange, Britain would send the colonies *finished products.*
   a. The British made things in factories (such as clothing made out of cotton) and sent them to the colonists.
   b. The British sent the colonists things they were finished with and did not need anymore.
   c. The British wanted the colonists to stop using all their products.

5. Americans often speak of their Puritan *heritage.*
   a. They are talking about their families.
   b. They are talking about buildings built by the Puritans.
   c. They are talking about ideas which have come to them from the past.

6. Having a common language has been a strong *tie* between the two nations.
   a. It has kept the nations together.
   b. It has caused problems between them.
   c. It has not made a difference in their relationship.

7. The Indians have asked the U.S. government to return land which was taken from their *ancestors.*
   a. people in their family who lived long ago
   b. people in their family who are living today
   c. people who were their enemies

8. In the fifty years from 1850 to 1900, the population *tripled.*
   a. It grew to twice its original size.
   b. It grew to three times its original size.
   c. It stayed the same.

9. At times there have been *anti*-Catholic and *anti*-Jewish groups.
   a. These groups welcomed the Catholics and Jews.
   b. These groups wanted more Catholics and Jews to come.
   c. These groups did not like Catholics and Jews.

10. But *so far,* this has not happened.
    a. today
    b. until now
    c. in the future

C. Choose the word form which correctly completes each sentence. Put verbs into the correct tense and voice. If necessary, make nouns plural.

1. immigrant, immigration, to immigrate
   a. In the 1840s about one-fifth of the population of Ireland . . . . . . to the United States.
   b. This . . . . . . occurred because the potato crop was very small and there wasn't enough food in Ireland.
   c. About one million Irish . . . . . . came to the U.S.

2. colony, colonist, to colonize, colonial
   a. France established some of the largest . . . . . . in the New World.
   b. England began to . . . . . . the east coast in the 1600s.
   c. Many of the British . . . . . . came in search of religious freedom.
   d. During . . . . . . times, there was much trade between America and England.

3. establishment, to establish, established
   a. Some colonies . . . . . . as homes for certain religious groups.
   b. The . . . . . . of colonies continued into the 1700s.
   c. Bringing slaves from Africa was an . . . . . . practice during the 1600s and 1700s.

4. similarity, similar, similarly
   a. There are certain . . . . . . among the immigrants from Latin America.
   b. They all speak Spanish and many of their customs are. . . . . . .
   c. . . . . . . , they come from cultures where close family ties are important.

5. culture, cultural, culturally
   a. The immigrants who came to the U.S. after the Civil War were . . . . . . very different.
   b. Their . . . . . . heritage included differences in religion, customs, music, etc.
   c. What was important in one . . . . . . was not necessarily important in the other.

6. reservation, to reserve
   a. The Indians were eventually forced to live on . . . .
   b. These were areas of land which . . . . . . for their use.

7. ancestor, ancestry, ancestral
   a. The Indians lost their . . . . . . lands.
   b. Many of their . . . . . . were killed by the white settlers.
   c. The . . . . . . of most Americans is a mixture of several nationalities.

8. race, racial, racially
   a. Some of the . . . . . . which live in the United States are the Oriental, the Caucasian, and the Negro.
   b. New York and other large cities have . . . . . . mixed areas.
   c. At times there have been serious . . . . . . problems in the United States.

9. nation, nationality, national, nationally
   a. The French, the Germans and the Spanish are three of the many different . . . . . . living in the United States.
   b. Britain is, however, the . . . . . . which has had the strongest influence on American culture.
   c. Problems between the races have received . . . . . . attention.
   d. Efforts have been made . . . . . . to solve the problems.

10. slavery, slave, to enslave
    a. There was . . . . . . in America for over two hundred years.
    b. African . . . . . . were first brought to the British colonies in 1619.
    c. No other race . . . . . . in America.

D. Rewrite each sentence. Choose one of these vocabulary words for the words and phrases in italics. Put verbs into the correct tense. If necessary, make nouns plural.

institution	heritage
similar	culture
reservation	permanent
slave	native
immigrant	take an active role in
tribe	

1. The history of the United States is filled with stories of *people who came to another country to live.*

2. Britain wanted to establish a *lasting* trade arrangement with the New World.

3. Americans sometimes speak of their Puritan *ideas which have come from the past.*

4. The *organizations* of the British government and the American government are *almost the same.*

5. The British had a strong influence on American *ideas, art, music, writings,* etc.

6. Christopher Columbus named the *original people* he found in North America "Indians."

7. The North American Indians were divided into many *groups.*

8. The Indians were forced to live on *areas of land kept separate.*

9. The Afro-Americans came to the United States as *persons owned by another.*

10. In recent years, black Americans have *been more active in* American life.

E. Use each group of words to make a sentence. Add other words, but use the words below in the form and order they are given.

1. colonies, established, centers, trade
2. beliefs, Puritans, part, American heritage
3. common language, tie, between, nations
4. Africans, brought, America, sold, slaves
5. immigrants, caused, changes, American society

F. The following paragraph is a summary of the chapter. Fill in the blanks with any word that makes sense.

Most of the ancestors_____ the American people came_____ the United States as_____ . Colonies were established in_____ America in the 1600s._____ British established the largest _____of colonies. They had_____ greatest influence on the_____ history and culture of _____ United States. The native _____ Indians were pushed westward _____ the colonists. Eventually the _____ were forced to live _____ reservations. Black Africans were _____ to America and sold _____ slaves. After the Civil _____, immigrants came to the_____ States in very large_____ . They came from China _____ Japan and from southern _____ eastern Europe. They brought _____ customs and religions to _____ United States. In the _____ many Latin American immigrants _____. The mixing of so _____ different races and nationalities _____ sometimes caused problems. However, _____ of these many groups _____come one nation.

G. *Questions for Discussion and Composition.*

1. Read again the two lines of Philip Bailey's poem. Explain how America is a "half-brother" of the world. What are some of the good things and some of the bad things America has gotten from other lands? Have any famous people from your country gone to live in the United States (U.S.)?

2. Discuss immigration in your own country. Have many immigrants from other nations come to your country? Have they come from cultures similar to your own? Does your government have any limit on numbers of immigrants? Are immigrants from all nations allowed to settle in your country?

3. Why do you think *E. Pluribus Unum* was chosen as a motto for the United States? Should the U.S. government continue to limit the number of immigrants who come to live in America?

4. Compare America's population growth since 1800 with the population growth of your country.

5. What are some of the reasons why immigrants came to America? Would you ever consider going to live in another country? Why would you want to, or not want to?

6. What are some of the problems immigrants have in a new nation? What are some of the problems a nation has when it accepts large numbers of immigrants?

Section Two

A. Write capital letters, commas, and periods where they are needed.

the most recent large group of immigrants is the latin americans most of them have come from mexico puerto rico and cuba the mexicans have settled mostly in california texas and in other areas of the southwest the puerto ricans have settled in new york city and the cubans in florida these people have brought a new language spanish and a new culture to the united states

B. Use these words and phrases in sentences that clearly show you understand their meaning.

1. to have in common
2. raw materials
3. a strong tie (*or* to have close ties)
4. native
5. immigration
6. ancestor
7. to take an active role in
8. triple
9. eventually
10. so far

C.   *Chapter Outline: The People*[1]

Introduction: The United States—a nation of immigrants
  I. The British
      A. Their reasons for colonizing North America
          1. Trade
          2. Religious freedom
      B. Their influence on U.S. history and culture
          1. Puritan heritage
          2. Language
          3. Institutions and culture
  II. The native American Indians
      A. Their origin
      B. Their life in tribes
      C. Their life after the colonists arrived
          1. Movement westward
          2. Wars with settlers
          3. Reservations
  III. The Afro-Americans
      A. Their slavery
      B. Their freedom at the end of the Civil War
      C. Their movement away from the South
  IV. The immigrants of the late 1800s and the 1900s
      A. Southern and eastern Europeans
          1. Large numbers after the Civil War
          2. Different customs and religions
          3. Changes in American society

[1]See Introduction, page vii, for suggestions on how to use this chapter outline.

    B. Japanese and Chinese
    C. Latin Americans
 V. Conclusion
    A. Problems with immigration
    B. "Melting pot" idea

D. There are two types of outlines. One is called a *topic outline* and the
   other is called a *sentence outline*. The outlines on pages 18 and 34 are
   topic outlines. In a topic outline, the main ideas and supporting
   details are written as topics, or subjects. The ideas are written in
   phrases, *not* in complete sentences.

   In a sentence outline, the main ideas and supporting details are
   written in complete sentences. A sentence outline and a topic outline
   may contain the same information. The difference is that the sentence
   outline must have each idea (or *entry*) written in a complete sentence.
   In a topic outline, the entries must *not* be complete sentences.

   Below there is a sentence outline of this chapter. It contains the
   same information as the topic outline, in C above. Compare the
   sentence outline and the topic outline. If you read the sentence
   outline aloud (not saying the numbers and letters), it will make a
   summary of the chapter.

Sentence Outline: The People

Introduction: The people of the United States have come from many
different nations.

 I. The British established colonies in North America in the 1600s and
     1700s.
     A. They established colonies for two reasons.
        1. Some wanted to establish centers of trade.
        2. Others wanted to have religious freedom.
     B. The British had a great influence on the history and culture of
        the United States.
        1. The Puritans have given Americans a religious heritage and a
           belief in hard work.
        2. The British gave the Americans their language—English.
        3. The Americans kept many British institutions after they
           formed a separate nation, and their culture is also influenced
           by the British.
 II. When the colonists arrived in America they found native people
     called Indians.
     A. The Indians probably came to America from Asia 5,000 years
        ago.

B. They lived in separate tribes, each with its own language and its own leaders.
C. Their life changed greatly after the colonists arrived.
  1. They moved westward.
  2. They fought with the white settlers who took their land.
  3. They were finally defeated and forced to live on reservations.

III. The Afro-Americans are another group which had an important influence on American culture.
  A. They were brought to America as slaves.
  B. They were not given their freedom until the end of the Civil War.
  C. After 1900 many black Americans moved away from the South.

IV. In the late 1800s and the 1900s many immigrants came to the new nation.
  A. Many of these immigrants were from southern and eastern Europe.
    1. Large numbers of them arrived after the Civil War.
    2. Their customs and religions were different.
    3. Their arrival brought many changes to the American society.
  B. Large numbers of Chinese and Japanese also came.
  C. In the 1900s, there have been many immigrants from Latin American countries.

V. Conclusion: The United States has been greatly influenced by the immigrants.
  A. The mixing of so many races and nationalities has sometimes caused problems.
  B. The United States has not been a real melting pot, because many differences still remain.

E. Write a paragraph about the problems of mixing together people from different nations. First list your ideas in a simple topic outline:

  I.   Problems of mixing people from different nations
        A. _____
        B. _____
        C. _____

Begin your paragraph with a sentence such as:

The mixing of people from many different nations may cause problems.

Continue your paragraph by writing a sentence on each idea you listed in the outline above.

The Declaration of Independence

We hold these truths to be self-evident, that all men are created equal, that they are endowed by their Creator with certain unalienable rights, that among these are Life, Liberty and the pursuit of Happiness. That to secure these rights, Governments are instituted among Men, deriving their just powers from the consent of the governed. That whenever any Form of Government becomes destructive of these ends, it is the Right of the People to alter or to abolish it, and to institute new Government. . . .

We believe that these things are completely true—all people are born equal (God made all people equal). God said all people must have certain things. All people must have life; all people must be free; all people must have the chance to find happiness. Governments are made by people. These governments must help people live, be free, and find happiness. These governments must do what the people want. When a government does not do what the people want, the people can change the government, or they can end it and make a new government.

The Boston Tea Party

CHAPTER 3

THE AMERICAN REVOLUTION

I know not what course
Others may take.
But as for me—
Give me liberty
Or give me death!

Patrick Henry
(Virginia statesman and colonial legislator) 1775

The American Revolution began in 1775. In April of that year, at the British colonial town of Concord in Massachusetts, the first shot of the war was fired. The American writer Ralph Waldo Emerson later called it "the shot heard 'round the world." When that shot was fired, fighting began between the Americans and their mother country, Great Britain. It would become a war for independence, the Revolutionary War. The American colonies would decide to establish an independent nation.

The colonists had not always wanted to be independent. They had had close ties with Britain. But in the 1760s Britain began to increase colonial taxes. There had been a few taxes before, but they were often not collected. Now the British government needed the tax money to help pay for expenses in the colonies. The biggest expense was the British army.

During the war against the French and Indians (1754-1763), Britain had sent many soldiers to protect the colonists. Now the war was over, but the colonists still needed protection from the Indians, and British soldiers remained in America. Britain needed money to pay these soldiers and to pay for other government expenses.

The colonists did not like the new British taxes. Many believed that the British Parliament did not have the right to tax them. Each colony had its own legislature, and the colonists believed that their own legislatures, not the British Parliament, should make tax laws, since they had no representatives in Parliament. They believed they did not have the same rights as British citizens living in England. The colonists said they had "taxation without representation."

The British Parliament passed a number of tax laws.[1] In 1765 it passed the famous Stamp Act. Some of the colonists were so angry that they attacked and threatened the British tax collectors. Eventually the British removed almost all of the taxes, but they left a tax on tea. The British said that the tax on tea was important, because it proved that they still had the right to tax the colonies.

In 1773 some of the Americans in Boston decided to protest the tax on tea. They dressed like Indians and went onto some British ships on which there were large boxes of tea. The Americans threw the boxes of tea into the water. This famous act of protest is called the Boston Tea Party. There were other acts of protest. The Americans refused to buy British products and this angered the British.

Some of the American leaders tried to find peaceful solutions to the problems with the mother country. But the situation was becoming worse. The British sent more soldiers to America, and some of the Americans began to collect guns and other weapons. There was a collection of weapons at Concord, Massachusetts. In 1775, the British soldiers went to

---

[1] *to pass a law*: to make a law

get those weapons. Armed colonists were waiting for them on the road, and the first shots were fired.

Soon after the fighting began, a group of American leaders met to discuss the situation. The group was called the Continental Congress. It was made up of representatives from each of the thirteen colonies, meeting in Philadelphia, Pennsylvania. They decided to organize an army, and named George Washington as the leader of their small army. At the same time they tried to make peace with Britain. Most Americans did not want independence at that time.

As the months passed, however, the fighting continued. The situation began to look hopeless. Some Americans spoke strongly of the need for independence. In 1775 Patrick Henry gave his famous "Give me liberty or give me death" speech. John Adams, who later became the second President of the United States, wrote in 1775 that the colonial legislatures were the only ones with the power to govern the colonies. Thomas Paine wrote in 1776 that it was unnatural for an island (Great Britain) to rule a continent (North America). He said, "A government of our own is our natural right."

Finally the Continental Congress decided to declare America independent and to establish a new government. A group of representatives began writing the Declaration of Independence. It was largely written by Thomas Jefferson, who later became the third President. On July 4, 1776, Congress approved the Declaration of Independence. July 4th is still celebrated as Independence Day.

Jefferson was a political philosopher. In the Declaration of Independence, he explained why the Americans had the right to revolt against the British government. All people are created equal, he said. God has given certain rights to all people. Among these are the rights to "life, liberty and the pursuit of happiness."[2] Governments are created to protect these rights. When a government does not do this, the people have a right to change or to end the government. The Americans believed that Britain had not protected these rights—in fact, it had

---

[2]*the pursuit of happiness*: the search for happiness

taken away many of their rights. Therefore, the Americans had the right to revolt against the government and declare independence. They would create a new government which would protect their rights.

The Declaration of Independence has become one of the most famous documents in American history. The words are familiar to most Americans, and many school children have memorized[3] the first part of the document. Thomas Jefferson considered it to be one of his finest achievements.

The men who signed their names to the Declaration of Independence were men of wealth, high social position, and influence. They are called the "founding fathers" because they helped to found the new nation. Perhaps some of them believed they had much to gain from the founding of an independent nation. But they also knew that the years ahead would be difficult. If the Americans failed to win their independence, their leaders' lives would be in danger. One of the leaders, Benjamin Franklin, said that they must all "hang together" or they would surely all hang separately.[4]

The war for independence lasted until 1783. Some Americans who did not want the colonies to be independent left the country. Some of them went to England; others went across the border to Canada. The war killed many people, British and American. It involved several European nations, including France and Spain. It produced America's first national hero: George Washington.

George Washington was from Virginia. He was a wealthy farmer and a slave-owner. He was a practical man, and he did not ask philosophical questions. Washington led his soldiers through difficult times when the Americans had few weapons and supplies. It was very difficult to fight against the well-armed British soldiers. But eventually the British were defeated, and Washington was called a hero. The American people loved and respected him. After the war he became

---

[3]*to memorize*: to learn

[4]*to hang* or *to be hanged*: to be killed by being hung by a rope around one's neck

   to hang together: to stick together, to be united—in other words, if they were not united, they would certainly be killed.

involved in politics, and became the first President of the new nation in 1789. George Washington was one of the most famous and best-loved American Presidents. He had no children of his own, but he is known as "the father of his country."

The long war for independence caused much hatred between the British and the Americans. Some Englishmen did respect the Americans, however. William Pitt was one of these. He had been the leader of the British government during the French and Indian War. He thought it would be difficult to defeat the Americans. In 1777 Pitt warned the British, "You cannot conquer America." But many of his countrymen did not share his opinions; they agreed with Dr. Samuel Johnson, who said in 1778, "I am willing to love all mankind, except an American."[5]

The Americans certainly had little love for the British after the war. Indeed, most Americans were very anti-British. After they had won their independence, they continued to view Britain as the enemy of freedom. There was a second short war, from 1812 to 1815, between Great Britain and the United States. The memories of war continued for many years. Americans became less interested in their British heritage. There was less British influence on American culture and institutions. It was not until the 1900s that there were again strong ties between Britain and the United States.

When the Revolutionary War ended in 1783, the American colonies were free. But what would the Americans do with their freedom? What form of government should they establish? Winning the war for independence was only a beginning. Dr. Benjamin Rush said in 1787, "The American War is over: but this is far from being the case with the American revolution. On the contrary, nothing but the first act of the great drama is closed. It remains yet to establish and perfect our new forms of government."[6] There was still much for the founders of the new nation to do.

[5]"I can love anyone except an American."
[6]"The American war is finished, but the revolution is not finished. Indeed, only the first part of the play (or action) is finished. We must still establish and make perfect our new form of government."

NEW WORDS

a document   An important piece of paper.

to found   To establish; to start something new.

to have the right to do something   To be able to do something, with the knowledge and belief that one is correct to do so.

a legislature   The government organization which makes the laws.

EXERCISES

Section One

A. Circle the letter next to the best answer.

1. In 1775, British soldiers went to Concord, Massachusetts, because the Americans
   a. had thrown tea from British ships into the water.
   b. were keeping guns and other weapons there.
   c. were meeting there to establish a new government.

2. The Continental Congress
   a. was made up of representatives from the British government.
   b. was made up of representatives from each continent.
   c. was made up of representatives from each of the thirteen American colonies.

3. At the time the fighting began in 1775,
   a. most Americans wanted independence from Britain.
   b. most Americans did not want independence.
   c. no effort was made to find a peaceful solution to the problems between Britain and the colonies.

4. In the Declaration of Independence the Americans explained why
   a. the British did not have the right to tax them.
   b. all people are created equal.
   c. they had the right to revolt against the British government.

5. The men who signed their names to the Declaration of Independence
   a. were working men who had no special social position.
   b. were men who had money and power.
   c. were hanged by the British.

6. The Revolutionary War ended in
   a. 1783.
   b. 1789.
   c. 1815.

7. George Washington was *not*
   a. a political philosopher.
   b. known as the father of his country.
   c. the leader of the American army during the Revolutionary War.

8. After the Revolutionary War
   a. there was no more fighting between the British and the Americans.
   b. the relationship between Britain and America was bad until the 1900s.
   c. the close ties between the two nations were established again by the 1800s.

9. The author *implies but does not actually say* that the British eventually took away almost all the taxes because
   a. the colonists protested against them so strongly.
   b. they no longer needed the money.
   c. the British soldiers had returned to England by 1773.

10. The author *implies but does not actually say* that
   a. the colonists were not keeping guns and other weapons at Concord, Massachusetts.
   b. the British did not want the Americans to keep their own supply of guns.
   c. the Americans were collecting weapons to protect themselves against the Indians.

B. Circle the letter next to the best answer.
   1. Emerson said that the first shot of the war was *"the shot heard 'round the world."*
      a. It was very loud.
      b. All of the countries of the world heard the news of the war.
      c. All the American colonists heard about the war.

   2. The American colonies decided to establish an *independent* nation.
      a. They wanted their country to be important.

      b. They wanted a wealthy nation.

      c. They wanted to have their own government, separate from England.

3. The Americans said they did not *have the same rights* as British citizens living in England.
   a. They were not allowed to do the same things.
   b. The British government said that the Americans were wrong.
   c. The British citizens living in England did not have to pay taxes.

4. Each colony had its own *legislative* group.
   a. soldiers who protected each colony
   b. people who made laws for the colony
   c. people who collected taxes for the colony

5. *Armed* colonists were waiting for the British soldiers on the road.
   a. The colonists had guns.
   b. The colonists were angry.
   c. The colonists went to meet the British soldiers.

6. The Continental Congress *was made up of* representatives from each of the thirteen colonies.
   a. The representatives were forced to come.
   b. The representatives were happy to come.
   c. The Congress included representatives from each colony.

7. Governments are *created* to protect the rights of the people.
   a. made
   b. unable
   c. able

8. Jefferson was a *political philosopher.*
   a. He was not interested in politics.
   b. He was active in politics.
   c. He was interested in political ideas.

9. Franklin said that *if they didn't "hang together" they would surely hang separately.*
   a. If they did not work together, each one of them might be killed.
   b. If they were not killed together in a group, they would be killed one by one.
   c. If they did not work together, they would each have to work alone.

10. The Declaration of Independence says that all people have the right to life, liberty and *the pursuit of* happiness.
  a. being given
  b. searching for
  c. having

C. Choose the word form which correctly completes each sentence. Put verbs into the correct tense and voice. If necessary, make nouns plural.

  1. revolution, to revolt, revolutionary
    a. The American . . . . . . War lasted from 1775 until 1783.
    b. The colonists . . . . . . against the mother country, Britain, because they wanted to govern themselves.
    c. The French . . . . . . began in 1789.

  2. independence, to depend, independent, independently
    a. During the French and Indian War (1754-1763), the colonists . . . . . . on the British soldiers for protection.
    b. After the French had been defeated in North America, the colonists felt safer and more . . . .
    c. It was not until more than ten years later, however, that the colonists began to really think of living . . . .
    d. The idea of . . . . . . came as the British refused to listen to their demands.

  3. tax, taxation, to tax, taxable
    a. Some Americans believed that the British Parliament did not have the right . . . . . . them.
    b. They said they had " . . . . . . without representation."
    c. The British believed that they had the right to decide which products were . . . .
    d. They left the . . . . . . on tea as a reminder of their right to tax the colonies.

  4. legislature, legislator, legislation, to legislate, legislative
    a. Each of the American colonies had its own . . . . . . , called an "assembly."
    b. These . . . . . . groups were like little parliaments.
    c. The men who made up these groups were called . . . .
    d. They passed . . . . . . which was necessary for their colonies.
    e. They were not able . . . . . . agreements with foreign countries.

5. protest, protestor, to protest
   a. The Boston Tea Party was held . . . . . . the British tax on tea.
   b. The . . . . . . dressed like Indians and threw boxes of tea off British ships into the water.
   c. Other colonists used another form of . . . . . . ; they refused to buy British products.

6. pursuit, to pursue
   a. The Declaration of Independence says that all people have the right to life, liberty and the . . . . . . of happiness.
   b. There are many ways a person might . . . . . . happiness.

7. declaration, to declare
   a. The British and the Americans had been fighting for over a year before the Americans decided . . . . . . themselves independent.
   b. Their formal . . . . . . was made on July 4, 1776, now known as "Independence Day."

8. philosophy, philosopher, to philosophize, philosophical, philosophically
   a. Thomas Jefferson is considered one of America's greatest political . . . . . .
   b. He was interested in the . . . . . . of government and its relationship to the people.
   c. George Washington was less . . . . . . and more practical.
   d. He was more interested in doing things, in making things work; he did not . . . . . .
   e. . . . . . . , their views of the Revolutionary War were similar.

9. founder, foundation, to found, founding
   a. The . . . . . . fathers wrote the early documents which described the important ideas of the new nation.
   b. These documents are the . . . . . . for the American system of government.
   c. The nation . . . . . . on the ideas described in the Declaration of Independence and the Constitution.
   d. The . . . . . . of the new nation wanted to protect the rights of the citizens.

10. hero, heroism, heroic, heroically
    a. George Washington was a . . . . . . of the Revolutionary War.
    b. He is known for his . . . . . . leadership of the American soldiers against the British.

c. The Americans had few weapons and not enough supplies, but they fought . . . .

d. There are many stories of the . . . . . . of these soldiers.

D. Rewrite each sentence. Choose one of these vocabulary words for the words and phrases in italics. Put verbs into the correct tense. If necessary, make nouns plural. Add or change articles, if necessary.

independent	representative
legislature	tax
document	situation
to found	to protest
to involve	weapon

1. Many colonists believed the British Parliament did not have the right to ask them to pay *money to the government.*

2. Each colony had its own *government organization which made laws.*

3. The American colonists had no *people to speak for them* in the British Parliament.

4. Some of the colonists wanted to *speak or act against* the "taxation without representation."

5. There was a collection of *guns* at Concord, Massachusetts.

6. When the fighting began, a group of colonial leaders met to discuss *what was happening.*

7. The Continental Congress said that America should be *free and have a separate government.*

8. The Declaration of Independence has become one of the most famous *important pieces of paper* in American history.

9. Benjamin Franklin was one of the leaders who helped *establish* the new nation.

10. The American Revolutionary War *included* several European nations before it finished.

E. The following paragraph is a summary of the chapter. Fill in the blanks with any word that makes sense.

In 1776 the American _____declared their independence from_____ Britain. There were several _____ why the colonies wanted _____ independence. The most important _____was probably that the_____ did not want to_____taxed by Britain. The_____ government believed that the _____ should help pay for_____ expenses of protecting and _____ the colonies. When the _____ government began to increase _____ taxes, the colonists protested. _____ of the taxes were _____ removed. However, now the_____ felt more independent. The _____ tried to prove that_____ had the right to_____ the Americans. Some Americans_____ they did not have _____ right. Finally, they began _____ fight. Eventually the fighting_____ a war—the war _____ independence.

F. *Questions for Discussion and Composition.*

1. Why do nations establish colonies? Name some countries that have had (or now have) colonies. What has happened to the British colonies? Has your country ever had colonies? Has your country ever been a colony?

2. Discuss the idea of revolution. Has there ever been a revolution in your country? (What happened?) Do you have an independence day in your country? What happened in the French and Russian revolutions? When do you think a government should be overthrown? Would you ever fight in a revolution?

3. What kind of taxes do you have in your country? Who decides what the taxes will be and how much they will be? Is there a legislature in your country? Does it have the power to tax? Have there ever been protests against taxes?

4. Do you have a group similar to the American "founding fathers"? Is there anyone known as the father of your country? Were (or are) any of your government leaders also political philosophers? Name some famous political philosophers.

5. The American Declaration of Independence says that all people are created equal and that they have the right to life, liberty and the pursuit of happiness. Do you agree or disagree? Why? Does a government have the responsibility to help people find happiness?

6.   Are there any documents in your country about the rights of your people? Have you memorized parts of any documents about your country? Discuss the role of government in protecting people's rights.

Section Two

A. Skim the chapter to find the paragraph which tells about the Boston Tea Party. What is the first sentence of that paragraph?

Skim the chapter to find the paragraph where each of the following ideas is located. Write the first sentence of the paragraph containing the information.

1.   The explanation of the ideas of the Declaration of Independence.
2.   Why George Washington is known as "the father of his country."
3.   When the French and Indian War was fought.
4.   Why the colonists said they had "taxation without representation."
5.   Who went to the Continental Congress.

B. Use these words and phrases in sentences which clearly show you understand their meaning.

1.   to fire a shot
2.   to have the right to
3.   to pass a law
4.   to be made up of
5.   to hang together
6.   to be involved in (or with)
7.   to depend on
8.   to protest
9.   armed
10.   philosophy

C. Use each group of words to make a sentence. Add other words, but use the words below in the form and order they are given.

1.   American colonies, decided, establish, independent nation
2.   colonists, not like, new taxes
3.   group, leaders, met, discuss, situation

4. people have, right, change, government
5. founding fathers, helped, found, new nation
6. it caused, number, colonists, leave, country
7. Washington, was, hero, Revolutionary War
8. War, Independence, caused, hatred, British and Americans
9. Americans, continued, view, Britain, enemy, freedom
10. memories, war, continued, many years

D. The chapter outline in E (p. 53) is a sentence outline. The main ideas and supporting details are written in complete sentences. Below you will find a topic outline, which contains the same information as the sentence outline, but written in topic form. This topic outline is incomplete. All of the main ideas and some of the supporting details are missing. The missing entries are given but are not in the correct order.

 III. The fighting of the war
  I. The events leading to the war
  II. The beginning of the fighting
  A. The meeting of the Continental Congress
  A. The British taxation of the colonies in the 1760s
  A. The leadership of George Washington
  B. The colonists' protests against taxation
  B. The effects of the war
  B. The decision to declare independence
   1. Thomas Jefferson and the Declaration of Independence
   1. The hatred between the British and the Americans
   1. Leader of the poorly armed American army

Fill in the blanks with the topics above. When you have finished, compare this completed topic outline with the chapter outline on page 53.

Introduction: The beginning of the war for independence

I. _____

 A. _____
  1. Why the British needed the money
  2. Why the colonists believed the taxes were wrong
 B. _____
  1. How they protested
  2. Why they collected arms
  3. What happened when the British went to get the colonists' arms

II. _____

   A. _____

      1. The organization of an army
      2. The efforts to make peace
      3. The call for independence

   B. _____

      1. _____
      2. The role of the founding fathers

III. _____

   A. _____

      1. _____
      2. First President of the new nation

   B. _____

      1. _____
      2. Conclusion: the need to establish a new, independent government.

E.   *Chapter Outline: The American Revolution*[1]

Introduction: The Americans began fighting for their independence from Great Britain in 1775.

I.   There were several events which led to the war between Britain and her American colonies.
   A. The British began to increase the taxes of the colonists in the 1760s.
      1. They needed the money to pay for the expenses of protecting and governing America.
      2. Some colonists believed that the British Parliament had no right to tax them.
   B. Some of the colonists protested against the taxation.
      1. They protested by attacking the British tax collectors, destroying tea and refusing to buy British products.
      2. They began to collect weapons to prepare to fight.
      3. The British went to get these weapons and shots were fired.

---

[1]See Introduction, page vii, for suggestions on how to use this chapter outline.

II.   When the fighting began, the colonial leaders met to discuss the situation.
   A. Each colony sent representatives to the Continental Congress.
      1. They decided to organize an army.
      2. They continued to try to make peace with Britain.
      3. Some leaders called for independence from Britain.
   B. The colonists decided to declare independence on July 4, 1776.
      1. In the Declaration of Independence, Thomas Jefferson explained that the Americans had the right to revolt against the government.
      2. The founding fathers signed the document and the new nation began.

III. The War for independence lasted until 1783.
   A. The American army was led by George Washington.
      1. The American army had few weapons and supplies and it was difficult to defeat the British.
      2. George Washington became the first President of the new nation in 1789.
   B. The effects of the war continued after it ended in 1783.
      1. The British and the Americans disliked each other and did not re-establish close ties until the 1900s.
      2. Conclusion: Although the war had ended, the leaders still had work to do to establish a new, independent government.

The Preamble[1] to the Constitution

We, the people of the United States, in order to form a more perfect union, establish justice, insure domestic tranquility, provide for the common defense, promote the general welfare, and secure the blessings of liberty to ourselves and our posterity, do ordain and establish this Constitution for the United States of America.

We, the people of the United States, want a more perfect union of the states. We want to have justice and peace in our country. We want to be able to protect our nation. We want all our people to be healthy and happy. We want freedom for ourselves and our children forever. To do these things, we establish this Constitution for the United States of America.

[1]*a preamble*: an introduction

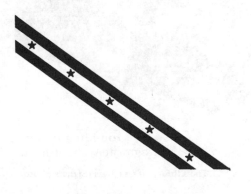

The founding fathers
sign the Constitution

The Library of Congress (Signers photo)

CHAPTER 4

THE CONSTITUTION AND THE GOVERNMENT

"I doubt whether any other Convention[2] will be able to make a better Constitution."

Benjamin Franklin
(one of the founding fathers) 1787

The first independent government of the United States began in 1781, before the Revolutionary War had ended, when a document called the Articles of Confederation[3] united the states into one nation. The fight for independence from Great Britain had been long and hard, so that the thirteen former colonies—now states—were left with a deep dislike of any strong national government, even one of their own. The Articles of Confederation established a very weak national government. Many American leaders believed that the government was too weak to keep the states together.

Eventually, a number of the leaders agreed that the new nation needed a stronger government. In 1787 they decided to

---

[2] *a convention*: meeting of a group

[3] *Articles of Confederation*: The rules by which the separate states were united into one nation.

meet in Philadelphia to make changes in the Articles of Confederation. Each of the thirteen states sent representatives to the meeting. They decided to do more than just make small changes in the Articles of Confederation. They decided to write a completely new Constitution, which would establish the supremacy of the national government over the state governments. The new Constitution was daring. It created a completely new system of government. Some of the representatives were surprised and unhappy about the new Constitution, but others were very enthusiastic. One of them said that he believed it was "the best form of government ever offered to the world."

The new Constitution declared that this document and the national system of government which it described would be "the supreme law of the land." The Articles of Confederation had left most of the power in the hands of the states. The new Constitution made the national government supreme: the states would have to obey the national laws.

The founding fathers wanted the national government to be powerful, but they did not want it to be too powerful. They thought that if the national government were too powerful, it could threaten freedom. Thomas Burke said that unlimited power cannot be safely given to any person or group of people. If all of the power were put in the hands of one part of the government, that part would be too strong. For this reason, the founding fathers separated the government into three branches.[4] They gave each branch important powers. One branch of government might threaten the freedom of the people; but the other branches would have enough power to check[5] it. And so the power would be balanced. The separation of power would protect freedom by what is called a system of "checks and balances" throughout the government.

The Constitution therefore divides the government of the United States into three separate branches: the legislative, the executive and the judicial. The three branches depend on each other, but no branch should control any other. The first

[4]*a branch*: a separate part
[5]*to check*: to stop, to prevent

branch, the legislative, is Congress. Congress makes the laws, and it also controls the money. It decides what taxes will be collected, and how this tax money will be spent by the national government. Perhaps its control over money is Congress's most important power.

Congress is divided into two houses—the House of Representatives and the Senate. The members of the House of Representatives are called representatives or congressmen. Representatives are elected for two-year terms. Each state has a different number of representatives, depending on the size of the population of the state: states which have large populations have many representatives, while those with smaller populations have fewer representatives. Today, for example, California, with the largest state population in the country, has 43 representatives, while Vermont, one of the smallest states, has only one representative.

The other house of Congress is the Senate. The members of the Senate are called senators, and they are elected for six-year terms. Each state has two senators. The size of the state's population makes no difference: California and Vermont each have two senators. All the states, large and small, have equal representation in the Senate.

The President is the leader of the second branch of the government, the executive. He[6] is called the "Chief Executive," and is elected for a four-year term. The Constitution makes him the leader of all the armed forces of the United States. It also says that he must execute the laws passed by Congress. The President must sign his name on each piece of legislation, or bill. Then the bill becomes law. The President does not have to sign a bill, however. If he does not believe it is good for the country, he can refuse to sign the bill; that is, he can veto the bill. His power to veto bills checks the power of Congress. However, Congress can try again to pass a bill which the President has vetoed. If two-thirds of both houses of Congress vote to pass the bill, it becomes law without the President's signature. Some Presidents have used the veto more

---

[6]Although the U.S. has not yet had a woman elected President, women may be elected to any public office, including the presidency.

than others. For example, Presidents Gerald Ford and Richard Nixon vetoed a large number of bills. They believed that Congress was spending too much money, and they vetoed many bills which would have caused the government to spend more money.

Congress has the power to pass laws; the President has the power to veto them. This is an example of how the system of checks and balances works. There are many more examples. Generally, whenever the founding fathers gave Congress a power, they gave the President a power to check it, and vice versa.[7]

The third branch of the national government is the judicial branch, which is made up of the system of national courts. The highest court is called the Supreme Court. The Supreme Court building is in Washington, D.C., across the street from the Capitol building, where the Senate and the House of Representatives meet.

The Supreme Court is made up of nine judges who serve on the Supreme Court for life. Some of them serve for many years. The President chooses the judges, but the Senate must approve his choices. The judges have the power to explain the meaning of the Constitution for Americans today. They decide if a law is constitutional or unconstitutional; that is, they decide whether or not a law is permitted by the Constitution. Sometimes their decisions surprise Americans. Recently the Supreme Court ruled that a woman has the right to have an abortion.[8] They also ruled that capital punishment[9] is generally unconstitutional.

The American leaders are elected by the people. If they do not do a good job, they are usually not re-elected. But if they use their power to do something wrong, they may be taken out of office. The procedure for taking an elected official out of office is called impeachment. When a person is impeached, s/he is accused of doing something wrong. Impeachment is a

---

[7]*vice versa*: The opposite is also true.

[8]*to have an abortion*: To end a pregnancy before a baby is born.

[9]*capital punishment*: Killing a person as punishment for a crime.

very special procedure and it is used very, very seldom. Both houses of Congress must vote in the procedure to impeach a President. No President has ever been taken out of office by impeachment, but it almost happened to President Andrew Johnson in 1868. More recently, there was talk of impeaching President Richard Nixon. The people and their representatives in Congress believed that Nixon had used his power wrongly. President Nixon resigned his office in August, 1974. He is the only President to have done so. If he had not resigned, he might have been impeached and forced to leave office.

The men who wrote the Constitution are remembered for establishing the supremacy of the national government over the state governments, and for their separation of the powers of the three branches of government. They believed this would protect the freedom of the American people.

Other leaders of the new nation believed that the Constitution did not do enough to protect freedom. They wanted to change the Constitution. The writers of the Constitution had planned a procedure for making such changes. The Constitution can be changed by adding amendments. Congress passes amendments to the Constitution, which must then be approved by three-quarters of the states.

The first Congress made ten amendments to the Constitution as soon as the new government began. The first ten amendments are called the "Bill of Rights." These amendments protect the citizens' right to freedom—freedom of speech, freedom of the press,[10] and freedom of religion. They also protect their right to a fair criminal trial. For example, Americans have the right to have a lawyer speak for them during a trial, and the right to a trial by jury. And citizens may not be tried twice for the same crime.

The Tenth Amendment protects the state governments against the power of the national government. Some of the early leaders were afraid that the strong new national government might destroy the state governments. The Tenth Amendment says that all the powers not given to the national

---

[10]*the press*: newspapers, magazines, books, etc.

government by the Constitution must be left to the states and the people.

Now, almost two hundred years later, the national government has certainly not destroyed the state governments. In 1789 there were thirteen states; that number has grown to fifty. They still have their own legislatures which make state laws. Today the states provide many important services in America. They provide most of the public education, and most of the law enforcement by police and courts.

The United States Constitution was not intended to create a democracy. It was created by wealthy, well-educated men of high social position. These founding fathers feared democracy almost as much as they feared monarchy. They wanted something between the two, something they called a "republic."

The founding fathers wanted the people to have a voice in[11] all three branches of their government, but they wanted to limit this voice. The people were allowed to elect only the members of the House of Representatives: the senators and the President were chosen differently. The people would elect their state legislators, who would choose the two senators from each state. Similarly, the people of each state would choose "electors" who would then choose the President.

The ideas and the practices of democracy have developed very slowly. The founding fathers feared too much democracy, but they did not want to destroy it, and they did not want to prevent democracy from developing in the future. Thomas Jefferson, the third President, believed that it was safe to have a more democratic government. He wrote in 1816, "I am not among those who fear the people." Andrew Jackson, the seventh President (1829-1836), believed that ordinary people could understand the government, and could take an active role in it.

America is not a pure democracy even today, but it is moving in that direction. There have been several important amendments to the Constitution in the twentieth century. For example, in 1913 the Seventeenth Amendment provided that

---

[11] *to have a voice in*: To have some power over.

the United States senators be elected directly by the people, instead of by their state legislators. The Nineteenth Amendment (1920) gave women the right to vote. The Twenty-Sixth Amendment (1971) lowered the voting age from twenty-one to eighteen.

The President is still elected by electors chosen by the people, but today the electors do not follow their own wishes, but those of the people. Electors today almost always vote for the person who gets the most votes from the people in their state.

The founding fathers would probably be surprised to see how much the United States has grown and changed—but they would be pleased, too. The government they created is still working under the Constitution they wrote almost two hundred years ago.

NEW WORDS

an amendment   A change.

a bill   A suggested law; a plan for a new law.

to elect   To vote into office.

impeachment   The procedure for taking an elected official out of office because s/he is believed to have done something wrong.

judicial   The part of the government that judges the law; the national courts.

to veto   To say no to; to refuse to sign a bill.

EXERCISES

Section One

A. Circle the letter next to the best answer.

1. When the representatives from each state met in Philadelphia, they decided to
    a. write a completely new Constitution.
    b. make small changes in the Articles of Confederation.
    c. make many changes in the Articles of Confederation.

2. The founding fathers separated the government into three parts because
   a. they did not want all of the power to be in one part.
   b. they believed the country was too large to be ruled by one branch of government.
   c. a government with three parts could be supreme.

3. The members of the United States Congress
   a. are called electors.
   b. are called senators and representatives.
   c. are called state legislators.

4. The size of a state's population makes a difference in the number of representatives it has in
   a. the Senate.
   b. the House of Representatives.
   c. the Supreme Court.

5. The President is the leader of
   a. the legislative branch of government.
   b. the judicial branch.
   c. the executive branch.

6. If Congress passes a bill the President does not like
   a. he must sign it into law.
   b. he does not have to sign it.
   c. the Supreme Court may force him to sign it.

7. The author *implies but does not actually say* that
   a. it is easy for Congress to pass bills the President does not like.
   b. it is necessary for the President and the Congress to work together to create new laws.
   c. the President has more power to make laws than Congress does.

8. If a U.S. President uses his power to do something wrong
   a. there is nothing to do but wait until the next election and vote him out of office.
   b. he may not be tried for a crime while he is in office.
   c. he may be removed from office by a special procedure called impeachment.

9. The Constitution of the United States
   a. can never be changed.
   b. can be changed.
   c. can be changed, but it never has been.

10. The Bill of Rights refers to
    a. a document written by the first President.
    b. the first ten amendments to the Constitution.
    c. a document written before the Constitution.

B. Circle the letter next to the best answer.

1. The Constitution established the *supremacy* of the national government over the state governments.
   a. The state governments would be more powerful than the national government.
   b. The national government would have power over the state governments.
   c. The national government would have to obey the state governments.

2. There is a system of *checks and balances* throughout the United States government.
   a. The government checks the money.
   b. The power of the government is divided so that one branch can stop another from taking all the power.
   c. The power is balanced between the government and the people.

3. Members of the House of Representatives are elected for two-year *terms* of office.
   a. They may be elected two times.
   b. There are elections twice a year.
   c. There are elections every two years.

4. The President has the power to *veto* bills.
   a. to refuse to sign a bill
   b. to make a bill become law
   c. to suggest bills to Congress

5. The President is Commander in Chief of the *armed forces* of the United States.
   a. He is the leader of the Army.
   b. He defends the nation against enemies.
   c. He has the highest responsibility for the Army, Navy, Marines, etc.

6. Generally, whenever the founding fathers gave Congress a power, they gave the President a power to check it, and *vice versa.*
   a. and so on
   b. and the opposite is true
   c. and this is true today

7. The justices of the Supreme Court serve *for life.*
   a. They give their lives to the Supreme Court.
   b. They must not earn any money from other jobs.
   c. They may continue to serve until they decide to resign, or until they die.

8. The Constitution protects the freedom of the *press.*
   a. the freedom to have a lawyer in court
   b. the freedom to write what you want, especially in the newspapers
   c. the freedom to have different religious beliefs

9. The founding fathers wanted the people to *have a voice in* all three branches of their government.
   a. They wanted people to talk about their government.
   b. They wanted people to respect all three branches.
   c. They wanted leaders in all three branches to listen to the opinions of the people.

10. The electors almost always *follow the wishes* of the people who have voted in their state.
   a. They vote for the President after the people have voted.
   b. They vote for the person they want to.
   c. They vote for the person the people want.

C. Choose the word form which correctly completes each sentence. Put verbs into the correct tense. If necessary, make nouns plural.

1. Constitution, constitutionality, constitutional
   a. The United States . . . . . . went into effect in 1789.

    b. The Supreme Court rules on the . . . . . . of laws.

    c. If a law is . . . . . . , it is allowed by the Constitution.

2. supremacy, supreme, supremely
   a. The Constitution is the . . . . . . law of the land.
   b. The founding fathers wanted to establish the . . . . . . of the national government over the state governments.
   c. They did not, however, want the government to rule so . . . . . . that it did not follow the wishes of the people.

3. system, systematic, systematically
   a. The writers of the Constitution described the three branches of government and how the new . . . . . . of government would work.
   b. They described each branch . . . .
   c. They gave a . . . . . . description of the powers of each branch.

4. check, to check
   a. The separation of powers provided that each of the branches of government could . . . . . . the power of the other.
   b. There is a system of . . . . . . and balances throughout the government.

5. impeachment, to impeach, impeachable
   a. A President may be taken out of office by a special procedure called . . . .
   b. The House of Representatives . . . . . . him by accusing him of wrong-doing.
   c. He is then tried by the Senate, which must decide if he is guilty of an . . . . . . action.

6. amendment, to amend
   a. The writers of the Constitution provided for a procedure . . . . . . the document.
   b. There have been more than twenty-five constitutional . . . . . . over its two-hundred year history.

7. democracy, democratic, democratically
   a. The United States is a representative . . . .
   b. The . . . . . . form of government has developed slowly over the last two hundred years.
   c. The government leaders are chosen more . . . . . . now than when the Constitution went into effect in 1789.

8. President, presidency, to preside, presidential
   a. There are . . . . . . elections every four years.
   b. The . . . . . . may serve no more than two terms in office.
   c. The Vice President . . . . . . over the meetings of the U.S. Senate.
   d. The . . . . . . as an office has become increasingly more powerful since World War II.

9. union, unity, to unite
   a. One of the reasons for establishing the new Constitution was "to form a more perfect . . . ."
   b. The states had been loosely . . . . . . by the Articles of Confederation.
   c. There was not enough of a feeling of . . . . . . , of belonging together.

10. elector, electoral, election, to elect, elected
    a. A President is . . . . . . every four years.
    b. On . . . . . . day in early November, the people vote.
    c. The people are actually choosing . . . . . . who will officially choose the President in mid-December.
    d. Each state has a certain number of . . . . . . votes, according to the size of its population.
    e. The newly . . . . . . President does not take office until the following January.

D. Rewrite each sentence. Choose one of these vocabulary words for the words and phrases in italics. Put verbs in the correct tenses. If necessary, make nouns plural. Add articles or prepositions, if needed.

amendment	veto
term	bill
provide	Constitution
executive branch	judicial branch
serve	sign
system	

1. The founding fathers wrote a completely new *document which describes the government and the important laws* for the United States.

2. The new Constitution created a new *organization* of government.

3. The President is the leader of the *branch of the government that carries out the laws.*

4. The Supreme Court leads the *branch of the government that judges the law.*

5. The President *writes his name on* each *piece of legislation* passed by Congress.

6. The President may *say no to* a bill he does not like.

7. The President is elected for a four-year *division of time.*

8. The Supreme Court judges *hold their position* on the court for life.

9. There have been more than twenty-five *changes* to the U.S. Constitution.

10. The state governments *offer* many services in the United States, such as public education.

E. Write capital letters, commas, and periods where they are needed.

the president does not have to sign a bill however if he does not believe it is good for the country he can refuse to sign the bill that is he can veto the bill his power to veto bills checks the power of congress however congress can try again to pass a bill which the president has vetoed if two-thirds of both houses of congress vote to pass the bill it becomes law without the president's signature some presidents have used the veto more than others for example presidents gerald ford and richard nixon vetoed a large number of bills they believed that congress was spending too much money and they vetoed many bills which would have caused the government to spend more money

F. The following paragraph is a summary of the chapter. Fill in the blanks with any word that makes sense.

In 1787, the leaders _____ the United States decided _____ write a new Constitution. _____ new Constitution created a _____ system of government. The _____ government had supremacy over _____ state governments. The powers _____ the national government were _____ and divided among the _____ branches of the government. _____ provided a system of _____ and balances. The three _____ of government are the _____ (the two houses of _____), the executive (led by_____ President) and the judicial (_____by the Supreme Court). _____ writers of the Constitution _____ democracy. They did not _____to give the people_____ much power. But they_____ for a procedure for _____ the Constitution by adding _____. By the two-hundredth birthday _____ the nation, in 1976, _____ total of twenty-six amendments _____ been passed. These amendments_____ helped democracy grow and_____.

G. *Questions for Discussion and Composition.*

1. Compare your country's form of government with that of the United States. Does your government have different branches? How is the power divided? Is there a system of checks and balances?

2. Discuss the Constitution of your country. When was it written? Who wrote it? What is the procedure for changing it? Has it been changed in your lifetime? Does it protect the citizens' right to freedom—freedom of speech, freedom of the press, and freedom of religion?

3. Compare the role of the President of the United States with the role of the leader in your country. How are they each chosen? How much power does each have? What is their relationship to other government organizations or branches? How can each be taken out of office?

4. Discuss the relationship between national governments and state governments. Are there state or regional governments in your country? How much power do they have? What services does each provide?

5. Discuss the court system of your country. Does a citizen have the right to a trial by jury? Who serves on the jury? Is a citizen accused of a crime considered innocent until he is proven guilty? Is there capital punishment?

6. Discuss the idea of democracy. How did the writers of the U.S. Constitution feel about democracy? How has the U.S. become more democratic since the Constitution was written? Do you think democracy is a good form of government? What are some of the problems of having a democratic form of government?

Section Two

A. Use each group of words to make a sentence. Add other words, but use the words below in the form and order they are given.

1. number, leaders, agreed, nation, needed, stronger government
2. 1787, they, decided, meet, Philadelphia
3. Constitution, created, completely new system, government
4. there, be, system, checks and balances, government
5. Constitution, divides, government, United States, three branches
6. Congress, divided, two houses
7. President, is, leader, executive branch, government
8. President, signs, name, each piece, legislation
9. Congress, has, power, pass, laws
10. third, branch, national government, judicial branch

B. Fill in the blanks with *the, a* or *an,* as needed. If none are needed, write an *X* in the blank.

_____Congress is divided into _____ two houses— _____House of Representatives and _____ Senate. _____members of _____ House of Representatives are called_____ representatives or _____ congressmen. _____representatives are elected for_____two-year terms. Each state has _____ different number of _____ representatives, depending on _____size of_____population of_____state: states which have_____ large populations have_____ many representatives; while those with _____smaller populations have _____fewer representatives. Today, for example,_____ California, with_____largest state population in_____ country, has _____ 43 representatives, while_____ Vermont, one of _____smallest states, has _____only one representative.

C.   *Chapter Outline: The Constitution*[1]

Introduction: The need to establish a stronger national government

I.   The Constitutional Convention
     A. The need to make changes in the Articles of Confederation
     B. The decision to write a completely new Constitution
     C. The creation of a new system of government
          1. The supremacy of the national government over state governments

---

[1]See Introduction, page vii, for suggestions on how to use this chapter outline.

2. The separation of powers
   a. Three branches of government
   b. System of checks and balances

II. The new system of government
   A. Legislative branch—Congress
      1. Senate
      2. House of Representatives
      3. Control over money
   B. Executive branch—President
      1. Commander-in-Chief of armed forces
      2. Leader of executive branch
      3. Power to sign or veto bills
   C. Judicial branch—courts
      1. System of national courts
      2. Supreme Court
      3. Power of Supreme Court to declare laws constitutional or unconstitutional
   D. Impeachment procedure

III. The protection of freedom and the development of democracy
   A. The procedure for amending the Constitution
   B. The amendments passed by the first Congress
      1. The "Bill of Rights"—personal freedom
      2. The Tenth Amendment—rights of state governments
   C. The founding fathers' fear of democracy
      1. The early limits on democracy
      2. The later move toward more democracy
      3. Conclusion: Important democratic amendments of the 20th century

D. The chapter outline in C above is a topic outline. Below, you will find a sentence outline containing the same information. However, some of the supporting details have been omitted. Looking at the chapter outline, fill in the missing details. Be sure to write each entry in a complete sentence.

Sentence Outline

Introduction: Many leaders of the new nation believed that there was a need to establish a stronger national government.

I.   The leaders met in Philadelphia at a Constitutional Convention.
A. They needed to make changes in the Articles of Confederation.
B. They decided instead to write a completely new Constitution.
C. They created a new system of government.
    1. _____
    2. They provided for the separation of powers.
        a. _____
        b. _____

II.   The Constitution described the new system of government, its three branches and how they worked.
A. The legislative branch is made up of the two houses of Congress.
    1. _____
    2. _____
    3. _____
B. The executive branch is led by the President.
    1. _____
    2. _____
    3. _____
C. The judicial branch is made up of the national courts.
    1. _____
    2. _____
    3. _____
D. There is a procedure for taking an elected official out of office; it is called impeachment.

III. Democracy has developed gradually since the writing of the Constitution.
A. The writers of the Constitution provided for a procedure for amending the document.
B. There were important amendments passed by the first Congress.
    1. _____
    2. _____

C. The founding fathers feared democracy and did not want to give the people too much direct power.

1. _____

2. _____

3. Conclusion:_____

E. The following paragraph tells why the confederation had a weak government. The phrases in italics show the important ideas.

The government established by the Articles of Confederation was a confederation, which had a very weak national government. There were three reasons for this. First, *each state wanted to keep its own independence.* The states were afraid of losing their rights if there were a strong national government. Second, the states agreed to unite only if *most of the power would be left in the hands of the state governments.* Finally, *the government had only one branch*—a national legislature, *a Congress with very little power.* It had no President; it had no executive branch and no judicial branch.

Here is a sentence outline for the paragraph:

I. There were three reasons why the confederation had a weak national government.
A. Each state wanted to keep its own independence.
B. Most of the power was left in the hands of the state governments.
C. The national government had only one branch—a Congress with very little power.

F. The following paragraph describes the problems of having such a weak government. The important points are written in italics. Read the paragraph and then complete the outline which follows it.

The weakness of the confederation caused a number of problems. First, *the national government could not enforce agreements that it made with foreign countries.* If a state government broke such an agreement, there was nothing that the national government could do. Second, *the national government was too weak to collect its own taxes.* To meet expenses, the Congress could only ask the state governments to pay their fair share. Finally, *the national government had no power to regulate business activities between states.* States would pass taxes to help businessmen in their own states, hurting businesses in others. There was no free trade between the states. Clearly, a stronger national government was needed for the new nation.

II. The national government of the confederation was so weak that there were many problems.

A. _____

B. _____

C. _____

G. Make a sentence outline of the branches of the government in your country. Reread the sentence outline of this chapter, on page 73, for ideas. Use the form below, and be sure to write complete sentences.

I. The government of my country has _____ branches.

A. _____

B. _____

C. _____

The Revolution for freedom and equality continues

Kearny and Baker

CHAPTER 5

THE CONTINUING REVOLUTION

I swear to the Lord
I still can't see
Why democracy means
Everybody but me.

Langston Hughes
(Black American poet) 1943

In 1776 when the Americans declared their independence from Britain, there was much talk of freedom and equality. The Declaration of Independence says that "all men are created equal," and that they have a right to "life, liberty, and the pursuit of happiness." But in 1776 there was a great difference between the ideals of liberty and equality and the actual conditions of life in America. Not all people were considered equal by law. Women were not allowed to vote. The Native American Indians were not considered citizens of the country. Indeed, not all Americans were even free. Almost all of the black people in America were still slaves. These three groups did not enjoy the same living conditions or have the same rights and opportunities that most white men had. For these groups, and others, the revolution continues.

Perhaps the Blacks more than any other group have made white Americans think about the ideals of liberty and equality. From earliest times, Black Americans have been an unhappy example of inequality in America. They were not freed from slavery until 1865 and their search for equal rights and opportunities still continues today.

The first African slaves were brought to North America in 1619, just twelve years after the British had established their first permanent colony in the New World. There were twenty Blacks and they were brought to the British colony at Jamestown, Virginia. By the middle of the seventeenth century, slavery had been established as a permanent institution. All of the African slaves who were brought to America after that, and all of their children and their descendants[1] were to be considered slaves.

The American Revolution did nothing to free the slaves. In 1776, when Thomas Jefferson wrote the words "all men are created equal" in the Declaration of Independence, few people believed that this included African slaves. And when the founding fathers met to write the Constitution in 1787, they did not want to discuss the question of slavery. They did decide, however, that it was necessary to count slaves among the population of the states where they lived. In the Constitution they wrote that each slave counted as three-fifths of a man.

In the late 1770s, slavery slowly came to an end in the northern states. The farms in the North were small, and slaves were not so useful there. The South, however, did not wish to end slavery. The southern states had large numbers of black slaves and a small white population. The farms were large and the growing season was long. The large southern farms were called plantations. The southern plantation-owners needed many workers to harvest the three important crops grown in the South—cotton, sugar and tobacco—and, by using slaves, they could harvest these crops very inexpensively. Many Southerners believed that slavery was not wrong. One famous

---

[1] *a descendant*: A future member of one's family.

southern speaker, John C. Calhoun of South Carolina, argued that slavery was actually good for African slaves. He said that it protected the Blacks while they were being "Christianized and civilized."[2]

Others, among them President Thomas Jefferson, argued that slavery was a crime against all people. Jefferson himself was a slave-owner, but he wanted his slaves to be freed after his death. Jefferson wrote that someday these people must be free, and other Americans shared his opinion. Some leaders of the new nation, including some Southerners, saw that slavery did not follow the ideals of the Declaration of Independence. Even at a time when few would argue that the black race was equal to the white, this was a contradiction.

For a time the nation lived with this contradiction. The South continued to use slaves to harvest the crops grown on plantations. The North accepted the fact that slavery was a part of the southern society. During the early years of the new nation, the number of slave states and free states was practically equal. But when Americans began moving toward the west, into the area now called the Midwest, things changed. The United States bought the Louisiana Territory from France in 1803, and in the early 1800s, this territory began to be divided into states. The uneasy[3] balance between slave and free states was suddenly threatened.

The Missouri Compromise of 1820 was a temporary solution to the problem. It admitted the new state of Missouri to the Union (the United States) as a slave state, and the new state of Maine as a free one. This compromise kept the number of slave and free states in balance. It also drew a line across the Louisiana Territory. In the future, all new states north of the line would be admitted to the Union as free states, while those that were south of this line would be admitted as slave states. This compromise was threatened, however, in 1848, when the United States added a large new territory in the Southwest,

[2]*"Christianized and civilized"*: Taught the Christian religion and American ideas of civilization.

[3]*uneasy*: uncomfortable

after a war with Mexico. Again there was a temporary solution, the Compromise of 1850. The North and the South were now close to a war over slavery, but the war did not actually begin until eleven years later.

The Civil War (1861-1865) finally decided the question of slavery in America when temporary solutions were no longer possible. The decades before the Civil War were a violent time. Movements to free the slaves were organized by such leaders as Frederick Douglass, himself a freed slave, and William Lloyd Garrison, a white newspaperman. The result was that many slaves tried to escape into free states on the "underground railroad." The underground railroad was a secret group of people, both black and white, organized to help slaves escape from the South to the North.

There were also a number of slave revolts during those decades. The most famous one was led by a Virginia slave known as Nat Turner, in 1831. It greatly frightened the Whites and made them tighten their control over their slaves. In 1859, just before the Civil War, a white man named John Brown tried to lead another revolt at Harpers Ferry, West Virginia.

In 1860 Abraham Lincoln was elected President. Lincoln was known to be against the idea of slavery in any new territories. He once said, "As I would not be a slave, so I would not be a master."[4] When Lincoln was elected, the southern slave states began leaving the Union. In 1861 these states established a new nation, the Confederate States of America, and the Civil War began.

After four years of fighting, the North won the war and the South returned to the Union. There were several reasons why the North won. It had more ships and a larger population, and it was far more industrialized than the South. It was certain that the South would eventually lose. However, because of excellent leadership and a strong wish to win, the South continued to fight until 1865. In 1863 President Lincoln wrote the Emancipation Proclamation, a document which ended slavery in the states that had left the Union. In 1865,

---

[4] *a master*: an owner of slaves

after the war had ended, the Thirteenth Amendment ended slavery everywhere in the United States.

The decades following the Civil War were difficult ones for black Americans. The Blacks were free, but they were not independent. Once they had worked for white landowners as slaves; now they worked for them as freedmen, but they were paid so little money that few were able to buy their own land and become independent. Moreover, Blacks had little voice in government. They were given the right to vote by the Fifteenth Amendment soon after the Civil War, but this right was protected for only a short time. White Southerners soon found ways, often violent and frightening ways, to prevent Blacks from voting.

Finally, there was the establishment of the practice of segregation. Segregation was the practice of separating Blacks and Whites in almost all areas of life, including schools, hotels, restaurants, and trains. Eventually segregation laws were passed in the South. The result of the practice of segregation was that Blacks were denied many opportunities that Whites enjoyed. In a famous decision, the U.S. Supreme Court said in 1896 that segregation laws did not deny the rights of Blacks. It said that Blacks could be separate from Whites and still be equal. Many believed that the idea of "separate but equal" was a contradiction, just as the idea of slavery in a free society had been. However, the Supreme Court decision of 1896 meant that segregation was legal. It was not until 1954 that the Supreme Court changed this decision, and ended legal segregation.

Although Blacks were denied many important rights and opportunities, they never stopped trying to improve their condition. One of their early leaders was a black educator named Booker T. Washington. In 1881, with the help of Northerners who gave money, he founded a college for Blacks at Tuskegee, Alabama. He did not choose to fight against segregation; instead, he spoke of self-improvement. He encouraged Blacks to remain in the South and learn new skills. In a famous speech called the Atlanta Compromise, he said that Blacks must have the skills necessary to earn money before they could ask for an equal place in society.

Other Black leaders did not agree with Washington's ideas. One of these was a college teacher with a Ph.D.[5] from Harvard University, named W. E. B. DuBois. DuBois said that any Black who listened to Washington's advice to stay in the South and learn skills would remain a second-class citizen.[6] He wanted to see Blacks thoroughly integrated with Whites in schools and in all other public places.

DuBois was the earliest organizer of the movement that later became the National Association for the Advancement of Colored People. The N.A.A.C.P. was one of the early leaders of the American civil rights movement. It went to court many times to protect the civil rights of Black people and it won many important court cases. The most important one was in 1954, when the Supreme Court ruled that segregation in the public schools was no longer legal.

World War II gave a large number of Blacks a new kind of freedom. Those in the army who went to foreign countries discovered a new way of life. Many of those who remained in the U.S. found jobs in northern factories which paid them more money than they had ever earned before. These wartime experiences encouraged millions of black people and gave them new hope for a better life. Less than a decade after the war ended, the modern civil rights movement began.

In 1956, the civil rights movement found the man who was perhaps its greatest leader, Dr. Martin Luther King, Jr. King had studied the use of non-violent demonstrations by Mahatma Gandhi in India, and he decided to use Gandhi's ideas in his fight for integration. In 1956 King led a successful attempt to integrate city buses in Montgomery, Alabama. Seven years later he attacked segregation in Birmingham, Alabama. There, in 1963, he led the largest non-violent demonstrations against segregation ever seen in America. Thousands of peaceful demonstrators walked through the city streets. White police-

---

[5]*Ph.D.*: Doctor of Philosophy, the highest degree one can get at a university.

[6]*second-class citizen*: A person who cannot get the best, or "first-class," things in life.

Civil Rights leader—
Martin Luther King, Jr.

The National Archives

men tried to stop them with police dogs and fire hoses.[7] Millions of Americans, including President Kennedy, watched these demonstrations on television. They saw demonstrators knocked down by the water from the fire hoses, and attacked by police dogs.

That year President Kennedy sent to Congress the most important civil rights bill since the end of the Civil War. The law said that racial segregation in restaurants, hotels, and other public places was illegal. This law was passed by Congress in 1964. In 1965, King led more non-violent demonstrations in Selma, Alabama. That year Congress passed a new voting rights law. Now that their right to vote was fully protected, black people began to have a voice in their government. King continued to lead the fight for equal rights for Blacks until he was assassinated[8] in April, 1968.

Blacks are, of course, only one example of the continuing revolution. A number of smaller minority groups in the United States are demanding equal rights, among them the American Indians. In 1970, President Nixon spoke to Congress about the problems of the American Indians. He said that the Indians

[7]*a fire hose*: A special pipe that bends which firemen use to carry water to a fire.
[8]*assassinated*: killed

were the minority group with the worst living conditions in the United States. On some of the poorest reservations, eighty percent of the Indians are unemployed. Their housing is poor and their health is bad. Many of the Indian children do not complete school. Three-quarters of the Indians who live in urban areas are poor. Organizations such as AIM (the American Indian Movement) are trying to help the Indians, but there is still much to be done.

Other minority groups are joining the fight for equal rights. One of the largest of these is the Mexican-Americans, the Chicanos, who are the largest minority group living in the Southwest. Many of them are migrant workers who travel from farm to farm harvesting crops. Led by Cesar Chavez, whose parents were poor migrant workers, they have won better working conditions from their employers in California. In the East there are large numbers of Puerto Ricans, especially in New York City. In Florida there are many Cubans. Like the Indians, the Chicanos, and the migrant workers, they want an equal place in American society. In several cities they have demanded better jobs, better education, and the use of Spanish as well as English in the public schools.

The largest group of all now demanding equality is not a minority group. It is American women, who form fifty-three percent of the population. When the black slaves were freed after the Civil War, women in America still could not vote. There were many demonstrations for voting rights. Finally, in 1920, the Nineteenth Amendment to the Constitution gave

Almost sixty years later, American women are still trying to end all forms of discrimination against themselves. In the 1970s, leaders of the women's movement demanded an "Equal Rights Amendment" to the Constitution, the ERA. This Twenty-seventh Amendment would prevent the national and state governments from discriminating against women in any way. Laws which now discriminate against women at work, in marriage, or in any other area of life, would be declared illegal. The intention of the ERA is to end all forms of discrimination against women in the USA.

No nation in the world has ever achieved perfect freedom and equality. Many have believed it was unwise even to try. Yet two hundred years after the Declaration of Independence was written, its words are still familiar to all Americans. Most Americans believe that these ideals are the foundation of a democratic society. Children are still taught to believe that the United States should be and perhaps can be a nation of freedom and equality for all people.

NEW WORDS

a compromise   An agreement between two persons or groups who have opposite opinions by which each side gives a little.

a contradiction   Something that says the opposite of something else.

discrimination   Seeing or making differences between; giving fewer rights to one group than to another.

to integrate   To mix together; here, the mixing of the black and white races.

migrant   Moving from place to place.

a plantation   A very large farm in the South.

segregation   The separating of people because of race.

EXERCISES

Section One

A. Circle the letter next to the best answer.

1. When the founding fathers met to write the Constitution in 1787
   a. they wanted to end slavery.
   b. they wanted to decide whether slavery was right or wrong.
   c. they did not want to discuss the question of slavery.

2. During the decades before the Civil War
   a. the slaves were freed in the South.
   b. there were a number of slave revolts.
   c. the question of slavery was not discussed.

3. When Abraham Lincoln was elected President in 1860,
   a. southern states started to leave the Union.
   b. he freed the slaves he owned.
   c. northern states established the Confederate States of America.

4. The Thirteenth Amendment to the Constitution
   a. ended slavery everywhere in the United States.
   b. ended slavery only in the southern states that had left the Union.
   c. gave black men the right to vote.

5. In the decades following the Civil War
   a. many black Southerners had enough money to buy their own land.
   b. white Southerners protected the Blacks' right to vote.
   c. segregation laws were passed in the South.

6. The N.A.A.C.P.
   a. was founded by Booker T. Washington.
   b. encouraged Blacks to stay in the south and learn new skills.
   c. went to court many times to protect the rights of Blacks.

7. In paragraph 13 (beginning *The decades following the Civil War . . .*) the author *implies but does not actually say* that
   a. White Southerners did not want Blacks to have a voice in government.
   b. The Blacks were not independent.
   c. The Blacks wanted to work in northern factories.

8. In paragraphs 19 and 20 (page 82) the author *implies but does not actually say* that
   a. The demonstrators fought with the policemen.
   b. The demonstrations led by Martin Luther King were non-violent.
   c. Seeing the demonstrations on television moved President Kennedy to prepare a civil rights bill.

9. The Equal Rights Amendment
   a. would make all laws discriminating against women illegal.
   b. would be the Twenty-first Amendment to the Constitution.
   c. would allow a woman to become President of the United States.

10. In the last paragraph, the author *implies but does not actually say* that
    a. the United States has achieved perfect freedom and equality.
    b. perfect freedom and equality do not exist in the United States.
    c. the Declaration of Independence was written 200 years ago.

B. Circle the letter next to the best answer.

1. The idea of slavery in a free society is a *contradiction*.
   a. It is an agreement between two groups who have opposite opinions.
   b. It is something that exists.
   c. The two ideas are opposites and one speaks against the other.

2. The Missouri Compromise was a *temporary* solution to the problem of slavery in new territories.
   a. The problem would be solved forever.
   b. The solution would continue into the distant future.
   c. The problem would be solved for a short time.

3. *Segregation* was practiced in the South for many years.
   a. Blacks and Whites were kept separate.
   b. The two races mixed together freely.
   c. Whites owned Blacks as slaves.

4. Blacks were *denied* many opportunities that Whites enjoyed.
   a. They enjoyed the same opportunities as Whites.
   b. Whites wanted them to have these opportunities.
   c. Whites prevented them from having these opportunities.

5. Booker T. Washington *encouraged* Blacks to remain in the South.
   a. He wanted them to stay there.
   b. He wanted them to leave.
   c. He did not have any opinion about where Blacks lived.

6. In 1776, almost all of the black people in America were still *slaves*.
   a. They were very poor.
   b. They had a good life.
   c. They were not free.

7. The *decades* before the Civil War were a violent time.
   a. The people were violent.
   b. The solutions to problems were violent.
   c. The 1840s and 1850s were violent.

8. DuBois said that any black person who listened to Washington's advice would remain a *second-class citizen.*
   a. S/he would be a good person.
   b. S/he would have very few opportunities for a better life.
   c. S/he could do anything any other citizen could do.

9. Some Spanish speakers have demanded the use of Spanish *as well as* English in the public schools.
   a. Spanish, not English.
   b. English, not Spanish.
   c. Both English and Spanish.

10. The Equal Rights Amendment would end *discrimination* against women.
   a. There would be no more public meetings of protest.
   b. Men and women would be equal by law.
   c. Women would have more advantages than men.

C. Choose the word form which correctly completes each sentence. Put verbs into the correct tense and voice. If necessary, make nouns plural.

1. encouragement, to encourage, encouraging, encouragingly
   a. Booker T. Washington . . . . . . Blacks to learn new skills.
   b. The Blacks had some . . . . . . experiences during World War II.
   c. The . . . . . . of the N.A.A.C.P. has been helpful to many civil rights groups.
   d. Martin Luther King spoke . . . . . . to the demonstrators.

2. contradiction, to contradict, contradictory
   a. In the American Black experience, the ideas of being "separate but equal" are . . . .
   b. The idea of slavery in a free society is a . . . .
   c. W.E.B. DuBois . . . . . . Booker T. Washington by advising Blacks to work for integration.

3. freedom, freedman, to free, free
   a. The slaves in the states that tried to leave the Union . . . . . . by the Emancipation Proclamation.

b. Some of the . . . . . helped other slaves escape on the underground railroad.
c. The Thirteenth Amendment to the Constitution gave the remaining slaves their . . . .
d. After the Civil War the Blacks were . . . . . . but not independent.

4. segregation, to segregate, segregated
   a. Legal . . . . . . continued in the South into the mid-1960s.
   b. It was legal . . . . . . the races on buses, with the Blacks sitting in the back part of the bus.
   c. There were even . . . . . . drinking fountains and restrooms.

5. integration, to integrate, integrated
   a. Children in the United States today go to . . . . . . schools.
   b. After the civil rights bill was passed in 1964, the South began . . . . . . schools, restaurants, parks and other public places.
   c. . . . . . . has not been easy for either Blacks or Whites.

6. compromise, to compromise
   a. When two people . . . . . . , they each give a little. Neither wins and neither loses.
   b. The North and the South made several . . . . . . over slavery, which prevented war for four decades.

7. temporary, temporarily
   a. A compromise may be a . . . . . . solution to a problem.
   b. During the demonstration, the street was . . . . . . closed.

8. demonstration, demonstrator, to demonstrate
   a. King studied Gandhi's use of non-violent . . . . . . in India.
   b. King told the . . . . . . that they must not fight with the police.
   c. Blacks and Whites together . . . . . . for equal rights for Blacks.

9. discrimination, to discriminate
   a. An employer is . . . . . . against women if he pays the men more money than he pays the women for doing equal work.
   b. Leaders of the women's rights movement want to end all forms of sexual . . . .

10. to legalize, legal, legally
    a. In 1896 the Supreme Court ruled that the segregation laws in the South were . . . .
    b. It said that Blacks could . . . . be segregated from Whites.
    c. As a result of another more recent Supreme Court decision, abortion . . . .

D. Each sentence has two words which have opposite meanings. Circle the word which correct completes the sentence.

1. This is only a (temporary—permanent) solution to our problem because it will not continue unchanged into the future.

2. Black Americans have been an unhappy example of (equality—inequality) in America.

3. Blacks, Chicanos and Indians are (minority—majority) groups in the United States.

4. After the Thirteenth Amendment, all the Black Americans were (freedmen—slaves).

5. In 1954 the Supreme Court ruled that segregation in public schools was (legal—illegal).

6. When they got high-paying jobs, the workers felt very (encouraged—discouraged).

7. When the African slaves first came to America, people thought they were (civilized—uncivilized).

8. The practice of separating Blacks from Whites is called (segregation—integration).

9. By using slaves in the fields, southern planters could harvest their crops very (expensively—inexpensively).

10. The black slaves, their children and all their (ancestors—descendants) were to be considered slaves.

E. Fill in the blanks with the correct words: *to, for, by, of.*

1. Women were not allowed . . . . . . vote.

2. . . . . . . using slaves, Southerners could harvest their crops very inexpensively.

3. . . . . . . a time the nation lived with this contradiction.

4. All new states north . . . . . . the line would be admitted to the Union as free states.

5. The North and the South were now close . . . . . . a war over slavery.

6. The slaves in the remaining states were eventually freed . . . . . . a Constitutional Amendment.

7. Booker T. Washington said that Blacks must have the skills necessary . . . . . . earn money before they asked . . . . . . an equal place in society.

8. The National Association . . . . . . the Advancement . . . . . . Colored People went . . . . . . court many times . . . . . . protect the rights . . . . . . black people.

9. Calhoun argued that slavery was good . . . . . . African slaves.

10. Other minority groups are joining the fight . . . . . . equal rights.

F. The following paragraph is a summary of the chapter. Fill in the blanks with any word that makes sense.

When the Declaration of_____ was written in 1776,_____ was a great difference_____ the ideals of freedom_____ equality and the actual_____ conditions of many Americans. _____ black Americans were slaves._____ ended in the North_____ the late 1700s, but_____ continued in the South_____ in some western territories_____ the end of the_____ War. After the Civil_____, segregation laws were passed _____ the South. In the_____, Martin Luther King led non-violent demonstrations_____ segregation. Congress then passed_____ ending segregation and protecting_____ voting rights. Other minority _____ have joined the fight _____ equal rights. Women also _____ to end discrimination against _____. The search for freedom_____ equality continues today.

G. *Questions for Discussion and Composition.*

1. Has slavery ever existed in your country? Do you know of any country where slavery is now legal? Do you think slavery has ever helped a country?

2. Are there any minority groups in your country? Are they denied any rights? What kind of living conditions do they have?

3. Can you think of any examples of discrimination in your country? Is there any discrimination against a group in your country because of race, religion, culture or nationality?

4. Discuss the place of women in your country. Are they equal to men? Do they have all the rights and privileges that men have? Can they vote? Can they own land? Can they work in jobs outside the home? Can they be government leaders? How has their role changed in the last twenty years?

5. Discuss the sentence "All men are created equal." Do you believe that all people have been created equal? Is it possible for any nation to have perfect equality among its citizens?

6. Discuss how change occurs in a society. What happens when a number of people are denied the rights that others have in their country? How can people end discrimination against themselves? Is great social change possible without having violence?

Section Two

A. Use each group of words to make a sentence. Add other words, but use the words below in the form and order they are given.

1. slaves, brought, North America, 1619
2. Blacks, denied, opportunities, Whites
3. slavery, free society, contradiction
4. crops, harvested, slaves, South
5. King, led, demonstrations, segregation
6. policemen, tried, stop, demonstrators, fire hoses
7. DuBois, believed, integration, necessary
8. slaves, freed, Thirteenth Amendment, Constitution
9. civil rights movement, began, decade, World War II
10. Puerto Ricans, demanded, use, Spanish, schools

B. Use these words. and phrases in sentences that clearly show you understand their meaning.

1. legal
2. living conditions
3. to discriminate against
4. to harvest
5. contradiction
6. compromise
7. decade

8. segregation
9. civil rights
10. demonstration

C.   *Chapter Outline: The Continuing Revolution*[1]

Introduction: The difference between the ideals of liberty and equality and the actual conditions of life in America in 1776

I.   The development of slavery
    A. When slaves were brought to America
    B. How Americans viewed slavery
      1. The writers of the Constitution
      2. The southern plantation owners
      3. President Thomas Jefferson

II.   The events leading to the end of slavery
    A. The attempts to keep the number of slave states and free states equal
    B. The attempts to end slavery
      1. Movements against slavery
      2. Slave revolts
    C. The defeat of the South in the Civil War
      1. President Abraham Lincoln's Emancipation Proclamation
      2. The Thirteenth Amendment to the Constitution

III.   The development of segregation in the South
    A. The attempts made by white southerners to keep Blacks separate
    B. The Supreme Court decision that segregation laws were legal
    C. The attempts by Blacks to improve their living conditions
      1. The philosophy of Booker T. Washington
      2. The philosophy of W.E.B. DuBois

IV.   The modern civil rights movement
    A. The changes brought about by World War II
    B. The civil rights demonstrations of the 1950s and 1960s
      1. The leadership of Martin Luther King, Jr.
      2. The use of non-violent demonstrations
    C. The civil rights laws passed by Congress
      1. The ending of legal segregation
      2. The protection of voting rights

---

[1]See Introduction, page vii, for suggestions on how to use this chapter outline.

V.   Other movements for equal rights
    A. The Indians
    B. The Chicanos
    C. The American women
    D. Conclusion: the American belief in freedom and equality

D. Reread the paragraph on page 78 which explains why slavery continued in the South after it had ended in the North. What are the reasons given? List the reasons in a simple *topic* outline:

    I. Why slavery continued in the South
      A. _____
      B. _____
      C. _____
      D. _____

E. Reread the paragraphs on pages 81 and 82 about Booker T. Washington and W.E.B. DuBois. The chapter outline lists their names and suggests that they each have a different philosophy about how to improve the living conditions of Blacks:

    C. The attempts by Blacks to improve their living conditions
      1. The philosophy of Booker T. Washington
      2. The philosophy of W. E. B. DuBois

Expand this part of the outline by listing what each man believed and did. Write each entry in *topic* outline form; do not write complete sentences.

    1. The philosophy of Booker T. Washington
      a. _____
      b. _____
      c. _____
      d. _____
    2. The philosophy of W. E. B. DuBois
      a. _____
      b. _____
      c. _____

F. Write a paragraph about minority groups in your country. Follow this topic outline:

I. Minority groups in my country
   A. Who they are
   B. How they are different from the majority
   C. What their living conditions are

Be sure to begin your paragraph with a good introductory sentence. For example: *The . . . . . . are one of the minority groups in my country.*

G. Write a paragraph about opportunities for women in your country. Follow this topic outline as you write.

I. Opportunities for women in my country
   A. Their education
   B. Job opportunities
   C. Voting in elections
   D. Holding government offices

Would you say there are many opportunities for women, or few? Begin your paragraph by stating your opinion in the first sentence:

There are many (or few) opportunities for women in my country.

Support your opinion with a sentence on each point of the outline. This paragraph could be expanded into a full composition.

The completion of the first transcontinental railroad

CHAPTER 6

BIG BUSINESS AND BIG GOVERNMENT

The contrast between the palace of the millionaire and the cottage[1] of the laborer with us to-day measures the change which has come with civilization.

Andrew Carnegie
(industrialist) 1889

The United States began as an agricultural nation. In 1782 Thomas Jefferson referred to the farmers as "the chosen people of God." As the nation grew in the early 1800s, some industry developed in the North, but the South continued to base its economy on agriculture. The defeat of the South in the Civil War (1861-1865) did more than end slavery: it ended a way of life. The Civil War destroyed the power of the South, which was based on agriculture, and gave power to the industrial North. An agricultural nation became an industrial nation, and the farmer was no longer the most admired American. By 1925, President Calvin Coolidge could say, "The business of America is business." The America that Jefferson had lived in and the one that Coolidge lived in were almost two different worlds.

---

[1]*a cottage*: a small house

The businessmen who became rich after the Civil War became very rich and very powerful. Few had dreamed of such wealth and power before the Civil War. Charles Francis Adams, whose father and grandfather had both been Presidents of the United States, described the changes. He had served as Ambassador[2] to England during the Civil War. When he returned to America in 1871, he was very surprised at the changes. He saw that a small number of businessmen had unbelievable power. They "controlled hundreds of miles of railway, thousands of men," and millions of dollars' worth of property. These new millionaire businessmen had the power to control courts, legislatures, and even state governments.

Probably the most noticeable of these men were those who made their money by building railroads across the nation. The railroads made it possible for people and products to move quickly across the continent. These men—men such as Cornelius Vanderbilt, Jay Gould, and Jim Fisk—fought each other for control of the new railroads. Once, some businessmen tried to take control of one of Vanderbilt's railroads. He wrote them a short letter:

Gentlemen:
   You have undertaken to cheat me. I will not sue[3] you, for the law takes too long. I will ruin you.[4]

                     Sincerely yours,
                     Cornelius Vanderbilt

Other men built empires in other businesses. Andrew Carnegie built the nation's largest steel producing company. John D. Rockefeller built an empire in the area of oil refining, buying many small oil refining companies and making one large company—Standard Oil Corporation. Rockefeller became known for his cruelty. He destroyed small companies which he could not buy. Andrew Carnegie once referred to Rockefeller as "Wreck-a-fellow."

---

[2]an Ambassador: official representative of the government
[3]to sue: to take to court
[4]to ruin: to destroy

Perhaps the most powerful businessman of the late nineteenth and early twentieth centuries was the banker, J. Pierpont Morgan. He lent money to businesses and then tried to gain control of them. At one time, he controlled 741 positions of leadership in 112 companies. One of his most memorable statements was, "I owe the public nothing."

Many of the new leaders of business were cruel and heartless men. They were certainly not the best-loved men in America, but by the end of the nineteenth century, they were the most admired. Americans had always believed in economic opportunity, and they had always admired a person who could use that opportunity to make money. This is a part of America's Puritan heritage, and it became strengthened as the settlers moved westward in the 1800s. The American people admired "rugged individualism." Each man was alone in the new, unsettled territories. He had to be rugged and independent. He had to have many skills. He had to build his own home, prepare his farmland, and protect himself and his family. The rugged individualism of these settlers is part of the American heritage, and it is still admired today.

After the Civil War, the new American business leaders were described in books and newspapers as "rugged individuals," using their business skills to make a stronger America. It is not surprising that to millions of Americans they were the new heroes. But if they were heroes to some Americans, they were villains to others. Most Americans probably had both of these contradictory feelings. They admired the business leaders, but they also feared and disliked them.

The farmers clearly saw the businessmen as villains and in the late nineteenth century they began to organize protest movements, especially in the South and in the Midwest and West. The farmer saw himself as a small, honest businessman. He believed that the men who owned the railroads were robbing him, because they were charging him too much money to take his products to market. There were other villains. The men who sold him his farm equipment charged him too much. The bankers who lent him money charged too much.

The farmer had another problem. The businessmen were putting companies together to form monopolies. A monopoly would control all, or most, of the trade in a certain product. One company might have a monopoly on certain pieces of farm equipment, for example. If the farmer wanted to buy this equipment, he would have to buy it from that company and pay whatever price the monopoly wanted to charge.

By the 1890s, millions of American farmers were well organized, and they decided to attack the empires of the big businessmen. The farmers had formed a number of protest political parties; the best known was the Populist or People's Party. One of the leaders of the Populist Party advised the farmers "to raise less corn and more hell."[5] James B. Weaver was the Populist candidate for President in 1892. He did not win the election, but he did win large numbers of votes in farm states in the South, the Midwest, and the West. Many were surprised at the numbers of people who voted for the Populist Party. It showed how angry the farmers were.

The factory workers in the cities protested against the power of big business also. Working conditions in the factories were far from ideal. The working hours were long and the pay was small. The factory workers were not as well organized as the farmers, but there was strong protest from labor unions at the beginning of the twentieth century. Two of the most famous leaders of the labor movement were Eugene Debs and Samuel Gompers. These two labor leaders disagreed with each other on the solution to the industrial workers' problems.

Eugene Debs was the president of the American Railway Union. He believed that the workers should take control of the factories and railroads. He believed that they should form their own political party, a Socialist Workers' Party, which would give the workers power "to conquer the political power of the nation . . . and make the workers themselves the masters of the earth. . . ."

Samuel Gompers, the president of the American Federation of Labor, disagreed. He said that the labor unions should support existing political parties. They should support whichever party would do the most for the worker. Gompers advised

---

[5]*to raise hell*: to make trouble

the workers to bargain with their employers and the political parties for better pay and better working conditions.

American workers and their labor unions have followed the advice of Gompers rather than Debs. They have bargained with their employers and they have become powerful. They have supported and influenced political parties. The Democratic Party has usually gotten the support and the votes of the workers and unions.

The protest against big business and powerful monopolies eventually caused the government to act. People demanded reform, and reform came. There was a national reform movement called the Progressive Movement, led by two American Presidents, Theodore Roosevelt (1901-1908) and Woodrow Wilson (1913-1920). In the past there had been little government regulation of business activities, but in the early decades of the 1900s government regulation of railroads, banking, and business monopolies increased.

Important reform laws were passed. Many Americans began to have a different view of the relationship between government and big business. They believed that Theodore Roosevelt and Woodrow Wilson were the first Presidents since the Civil War who were not controlled by the wishes of big business, but seemed to be listening more to the voice of the people.

The economic reforms were not enough, however. In the 1930s there was an economic depression, which is called the "Great Depression." It was the worst economic depression that Americans had ever suffered in a time of peace. There were many causes. One problem was that Americans did not have enough money to buy the products and services provided by American business. By 1929 the businesses had begun to suffer; they slowed down production or closed down altogether. For example, steel production dropped from 40 million tons in 1930 to 13.6 million tons in 1932.

As the businesses closed, workers lost their jobs. In 1930, four million Americans were unemployed. By 1932, twelve million were unemployed. Sometimes city governments provided work for low pay. If they said they needed 100 people, 1000 might come and ask for the work. Almost all Americans suffered.

Before the Great Depression most people believed that there was no need for national welfare programs to provide money or jobs, or retirement benefits. The individual did not need help from the government. The Great Depression changed these beliefs.

In 1932 Franklin D. Roosevelt was elected President. He believed that the government should provide economic support for citizens who needed it. During his first two terms in office, Roosevelt worked with Congress to pass many new laws which greatly increased the government's role as an economic provider. For the first time the national government took on the responsibility for helping people in need. The government would provide money for people who could not find jobs. It would provide payments for retired citizens.

These and other laws passed in the 1930s created what we call today "the welfare state." The creation of welfare programs caused the national government to get much bigger. Between 1933 and 1939 it tripled in size.

The leaders of big business disliked the new big government and its regulation of business activities. They especially disliked the man who was responsible for creating big government—President Franklin Roosevelt. The big businessmen considered him a villain. Most Americans, however, were basically pleased with Roosevelt's leadership and supported his daring new programs.

The economy greatly improved after World War II. The employment situation was much better. There were more jobs, higher wages, and better working conditions. At that time many Americans began to criticize big government and the welfare state: they did not like the taxes they had to pay to support them. Most Americans did not, however, want to destroy the welfare system. Instead, they wanted the government to spend their tax money carefully and without waste.

Many Americans today still criticize both big business and big government. Americans believe they have the right to criticize both institutions. They often disagree about what the role of business and government should be in their society. But they believe that, ideally, both business and government should serve the needs of the people. In January, 1977, Jimmy Carter became President. In his inauguration speech[6] he spoke of the need for good government. "Our government," he said, "must at the same time be competent and compassionate."[7]

NEW WORDS

a depression   A time of lowered business activity, not enough products for sale, low prices, and great unemployment.
a labor union   An organization of working people.
a party   A political organization.
rugged individualism   Being a strong or tough person.
a villain   A bad or evil person.
welfare   Government programs to give money and help to the people.

EXERCISES

Section One

A. Circle the letter next to the best answer.

1.   The United States became an industrial nation
     a. in the early 1800s.
     b. after the Civil War.
     c. after World War I.

2.   The businessmen of the late 1800s
     a. had all made their money by building railroads.
     b. controlled millions of dollars' worth of property but had little political power.
     c. were so rich and powerful that they could control state governments.

---

[6]*an inauguration speech*: The speech a new President makes at the time he officially becomes President (at his inauguration).
[7]*competent and compassionate*: do a good job economically, and also care about people

3. The powerful big businessmen of the late 1800s were
   a. loved by most Americans.
   b. admired by most Americans.
   c. hated by most Americans.

4. The idea of "rugged individualism" began
   a. during the Civil War.
   b. when Americans started to move westward into unsettled territory in the 1800s.
   c. when the businessmen of the late 1800s used their skills to make America strong.

5. The American farmers believed that
   a. the railroad owners were charging too much money.
   b. big businessmen were heroes.
   c. more railroads needed to be built to take their products to market.

6. The Populist or People's Party was supported by
   a. factory workers.
   b. farmers.
   c. railroad workers.

7. The farmer did not like the monopolies because
   a. they often did not have the equipment he needed to buy.
   b. he had to buy his equipment at whatever price they wanted to charge him.
   c. they had organized political parties to gain control of the government.

8. Samuel Gompers, a labor leader, believed that
   a. the workers should take control of the factories and railroads.
   b. the workers should form their own political party.
   c. the workers should support political parties which would help them.

9. In the early 1900s
   a. the American Presidents were largely controlled by the wishes of big business.
   b. the American government made no effort to control big business.
   c. the American government began to pass laws which would regulate big business.

10. Before the economic depression of the 1930s began
    a. there were many national welfare programs to provide money and jobs.
    b. people believed that government welfare programs were not necessary.
    c. most workers depended on government payments.

B. Circle the letter next to the best answer.

1. The South based its economy on *agriculture* during the nineteenth century.
   a. farming
   b. industry
   c. slavery

2. Some of the businessmen of the late 1800s were *millionaires.*
   a. They controlled millions of miles of railroad.
   b. They controlled millions of men.
   c. They had more than a million dollars.

3. The businessmen of the late 1800s were described in newspapers as *"rugged individuals."*
   a. They were tough, independent men who were using their business skills to build a strong nation.
   b. They were important men who had control of great wealth and power.
   c. They were men who were cruel and were only interested in gaining more wealth and power.

4. Businessmen were putting companies together to form *monopolies.*
   a. companies which controlled all, or most, of the trade in a certain product
   b. companies which would provide more products at lower cost
   c. companies which made a large variety of products

5. The new business leaders were *villains* in the eyes of some Americans.
   a. bad men
   b. good men
   c. men to be admired

6. Gompers believed that labor unions should *support* existing political parties.
   a. attack
   b. help
   c. protest against

7. Gompers advised the workers to *bargain* with their employers.
   a. He wanted them to have discussions with the employers in order to reach agreements.
   b. He wanted them to defeat the employers and take control of the factories.
   c. He wanted them to support their employers.

8. People demanded *reform.*
   a. equal rights
   b. a chance to earn more money
   c. a change to make things better

9. The government began to *regulate* business activities more closely.
   a. It passed laws which would control business activities.
   b. It tried to encourage the growth and development of businesses.
   c. It increased the taxes businesses paid.

10. The creation of *welfare* programs caused the national government to get much bigger.
   a. programs to regulate business activity
   b. programs to give money and help to people in need
   c. programs to help businesses

C. Choose the word form which correctly completes each sentence. Put verbs into the correct tense and voice. If necessary, make nouns plural.

1. agriculture, agricultural, agriculturally
   a. The United States began as an . . . . . . nation.
   b. . . . . . . is still important today, even though the nation is highly industrialized.
   c. The Midwest is an . . . . . . rich area.

2. basement, basis, to base, basic, basically
   a. Until the Civil War, the Old South . . . . . . its economy on agriculture.

    b. The . . . . . . of a house is the lowest part, usually under the ground.

    c. The railroad barons were . . . . . . interested in getting money and power.

    d. These men made their decisions on the . . . . . . of what would be good for them.

    e. The industrial revolution caused . . . . . . changes in the American way of life.

3. economy, economics, economist, to economize, economic, economical, economically

    a. A man who studies . . . . . . is called an . . . .

    b. The . . . . . . of the New South is much more varied than that of the Old South.

    c. The New South is an area where there have been great . . . . . . changes in the last few decades.

    d. The South is now . . . . . . varied and more independent.

    e. Small cars use less gas than larger ones, and they are therefore more . . . . . . to drive.

    f. People who want . . . . . . should drive a smaller car.

4. individual, individualism, individualize, individual, individually

    a. The idea of rugged . . . . . . comes from the days of the early settlers.

    b. In the United States, businesses are owned by . . . . . ., not by the government.

    c. Businesses which are . . . . . . owned are free to compete with each other.

    d. Teachers sometimes . . . . . . their teaching in order to meet the . . . . . . needs of their students.

5. equipment, to equip, equipped

    a. A well- . . . . . . American farm has many different machines.

    b. It takes thousands of dollars . . . . . . a farm with the usual machinery.

    c. Today, the farmer may choose to buy his farm . . . . . . from a number of different businesses.

6. monopoly, to monopolize

    a. The government has passed laws which try to prevent one company from . . . . . . the market in a certain product.

    b. A . . . . . . is a business which controls all, or most, of the trade in a certain product.

7. reform, reformer, to reform
   a. The business leaders had so much money and power in the 1800s that people began to demand . . . .
   b. Some . . . . . . were candidates for political office.
   c. President Theodore Roosevelt believed that the government should . . . . . . certain business practices.

8. regulation, to regulate, regular, regularly
   a. As a result of the reform movement, the government began . . . . . . business activities more closely.
   b. In the early decades of the 1900s, there had been little government . . . .
   c. The mailman delivers the mail . . . . . . every day.
   d. People depend on this . . . . . . mail service.

9. depression, to depress, depressed, depressing
   a. In the 1930s, there was an economic . . . . . . in the United States.
   b. Prices for farm products . . . . . . partly because farmers were producing too much.
   c. Men who could not find jobs became sad and . . . .
   d. The employment situation was so bad that looking for work was a . . . . . . experience.

10. retirement, to retire, retired
    a. Most Americans . . . . . . around the age of 65.
    b. There is a government program called "Social Security" which pays money to . . . . . . workers.
    c. Individual businesses usually have their own . . . . . . programs which provide additional payments.

D. Rewrite each sentence. Choose one of these vocabulary words for the words and phrases in italics. Put verbs into the correct tense. If necessary, make nouns plural. Add or change articles or prepositions, if needed.

monopoly	economy
support	agricultural
villain	reform
rugged	regulate
retire	labor

1. The United States began as a *farming* nation.

2. The *system of money, industry and employment* of the Old South was largely destroyed by the Civil War.

3. The settlers who lived in the new western territories had to be *strong and tough.*

4. The rich businessmen were heroes to some Americans, but they were *bad people* in the eyes of others.

5. The businessmen were putting companies together to form *business organizations with complete control over a certain product.*

6. There was also protest from the *worker* unions at the turn of the century.

7. Samuel Gompers believed that the labor unions should *give help to* existing political parties.

8. The farmers and the workers wanted *a change to make things better.*

9. The government began to *control* business activity more closely.

10. Most American workers *stop working* at age 65.

E. Write capital letters, commas, periods, and parentheses where they are needed.

the protest against big business and powerful monopolies eventually caused the government to act people demanded reform and reform came there was a national reform movement called the progressive movement led by two american presidents theodore roosevelt 1901-1908 and woodrow wilson 1913-1920 in the past there had been little government regulation of business activities but in the early decades of the 1900s government regulation of railroads banking and business monopolies increased

F. Use each group of words to make a sentence. Add other words, but use the words below in the form and order they are given.

1. Rockefeller, empire, area, oil refining
2. many, leaders, business, cruel
3. businessmen, heroes, eyes, Americans
4. powerful, movements, organized, South, West, Midwest

5. 1890s, millions, farmers, organized
6. workers, cities, suffering
7. government, began, regulate, businesses, closely
8. Presidents, seemed, listening, voice, people
9. individual, not need, help, government
10. Americans, not want, destroy, welfare system

G. The following paragraph is a summary of the chapter. Fill in the blanks with any word that makes sense.

After the Civil War, _____ United States changed from _____ agricultural nation to an _____ nation. A number of _____ became very rich and _____ powerful. They controlled railroads, _____ production, oil refineries and _____ . Most Americans admired the _____. However, some people suffered _____ of their power. The _____ organized political parties to _____ against the businessmen. The _____ formed labor unions which _____ with their employers and _____ existing political parties. Eventually _____ government began to regulate _____ activities more closely. In _____ 1930s, there was a _____ economic depression. The government _____ a welfare system to _____ unemployment and retirement payments. _____ today have both big _____ and big government.

H. *Questions for Discussion and Composition.*

1. Discuss industrialization in your country. When did industrialization begin? How much of your country's economy is now based on industry? Has the growth of industry been fast or slow? What changes has it brought to your society?

2. Discuss the role of the farmer in your country. How much of your country's economy is based on agriculture? How do your people view farmers? How much power do the farmers have? What kind of living conditions do they have?

3. Discuss J.P. Morgan's statement, "I owe the public nothing." What did he mean? Do you agree or disagree with his philosophy? What, if anything, do rich, powerful men owe the public? Who has the money and power in your country? How are these people viewed?

4. What is the relationship between business and government in your country? How much does your government regulate business activity? Does your government own any industries?

5. What kinds of payments does your government make to the people in your country? What things are provided by the government? Is education free? Is health care free? Are there payments to retired workers? How high are your taxes?

6. Describe the role of the factory workers in your country. How many hours a week do they work? What kind of working conditions do they have? Are there labor unions in your country? How much power do they have?

Section Two

A. Use these words and phrases in sentences which clearly show you understand their meaning.

1. ambassador
2. millionaire
3. cruel and heartless
4. to charge
5. to have a monopoly on
6. to support
7. to serve the needs of
8. to be based on
9. economic
10. inauguration speech

B. Fill in the blanks with one of these: *in, of, to, as, on*

The United States began_____ an agricultural nation. _____1782 Thomas Jefferson referred_____ the farmers_____ "the chosen people _____ God." _____ the nation grew _____ the early 1800s, some industry developed _____ the North, but the South continued_____ base its economy_____ agriculture. The defeat_____the South_____ the Civil War (1861-1865) did more than end slavery: it ended a way _____life. The Civil War destroyed the power _____the South, which was based_____agriculture, and gave power_____the industrial North.

C. *Chapter Outline: Big Business and Big Government*[1]

I. The development of big business
   A. Introduction: the change from an agricultural nation to an industrial one

---

[1]See Introduction, page vii, for suggested ways to use this chapter outline.

    B. The power and wealth of the new business leaders

    C. The Americans' respect for the businessmen

II. The protest against the power of big business

    A. The farmers' protest

    B. The workers' protest

    C. The government's reforms

III. The development of big government

    A. The problems caused by the Great Depression

    B. The solutions offered by the government

    C. Conclusion: the role of big government today

D. The chapter outline in C above can be expanded by adding more supporting details. Below is the first part of the outline, showing where supporting details can be added, numbered 1 and 2.

I. The development of big business

    A. Introduction: the change from an agricultural nation to an industrial one

        1. _____

        2. _____

    B. The power and wealth of the new business leaders

        1. _____

        2. _____

    C. The Americans' respect for the businessmen

        1. _____

        2. _____

The phrases below can be used to complete this part of the outline, but they are not arranged in the correct order. Recopy this part of the outline, arranging the supporting details in the correct order under A, B, and C.

> The American belief in economic opportunity
> The new power of the industrial North after the Civil War
> Other rich and powerful businessmen
> The defeat of the agricultural South in the Civil War
> The rich and powerful railroad owners
> The American belief in rugged individualism

Expand the rest of the chapter outline in this way.

II. The protest against the power of big business
   A. The farmers' protest
      1. _____
      2. _____
   B. The workers' protest
      1. _____
      2. _____
   C. The government's reforms
      1. _____
      2. _____

Recopy part II of the outline, arranging the supporting details below in the correct order under A, B, and C.

   The organization of labor unions
   The protest against high prices and business monopolies
   The passing of new laws to regulate business activity
   The organization of political protest parties
   The leadership of Presidents Theodore Roosevelt and Woodrow Wilson
   The protest against low pay and poor working conditions

III. The development of big government
   A. The problems caused by the Great Depression
      1. _____
      2. _____
   B. The solutions offered by the government
      1. _____
      2. _____
   C. Conclusion: the role of big government today
      1. _____
      2. _____

Recopy part III of the outline, arranging the supporting details below in the correct order under A, B, and C.

   The new government programs established by President Franklin Roosevelt
   The need for payments to retired workers

The creation of the welfare state
The Americans' criticism of big government and the welfare state
The need for jobs and money for the unemployed
The Americans' belief that government (and business) should serve the people's needs

E. Skim the chapter to find the four paragraphs about the labor unions and their leaders. What sentence introduces this part? Make an outline comparing Eugene Debs and Samuel Gompers, using the form below. You may write either a *sentence* outline or a *topic* outline, but do not mix the two. Include this information: the names of their labor unions, their beliefs, and their advice to the workers.

I. _____ (two labor leaders) _____

   A. _____ (name) _____

      1. _____ (union) _____

      2. _____ (belief) _____

      3. _____ (advice) _____

   B. _____ (name) _____

      1. _____ (union) _____

      2. _____ (belief) _____

      3. _____ (advice) _____

F. Write a paragraph following the outline you wrote about the labor leaders. Compare their beliefs and their advice to the workers.

Sign asking people to join the U.S. Army

CHAPTER 7

THE RISE TO WORLD POWER

The truth is I didn't want the Philippines and when they came to us as a gift from the gods, I did not know what to do about them.

President William McKinley, 1898

The role of the United States as a major world power is a fairly recent one. Throughout most of their history, Americans have believed that they could and should avoid the responsibilities of a major world power. Their first President, George Washington, advised them not to become involved in international politics. He said in his last presidential speech in 1796, "It is our true policy to steer clear of permanent alliances with any portion of the foreign world." Washington believed that the Americans needed time to develop their country. He thought that if the new nation were to grow and develop, the United States would have to steer clear of alliances with foreign countries, which might involve the United States in the wars of other countries. This policy became known as isolationism. For about 150 years the United States tried to isolate itself from the rest of the world as much as possible, making no peacetime alliances until 1949.

In the early years of their history, Americans were determined to avoid wars involving the great European powers, France and Britain. But American isolationism did not simply mean avoiding alliances with European nations. It also meant that the European nations should not interfere in the Western Hemisphere[1] (North and South America). In 1823, the United States declared that European powers should not establish any new territorial control in the Western Hemisphere; in exchange, the United States promised not to interfere in European politics. This policy became known as the Monroe Doctrine (after President James Monroe).

Luckily for the United States, Great Britain approved of the Monroe Doctrine, and was ready to help enforce it. Britain would stop other European nations from interfering in the Western Hemisphere, and it would send its powerful navy, if necessary. With this help from Britain, the United States established itself as a major power in the Western Hemisphere. In doing so, it gained Britain's support without having to make any alliance.

During the early 1800s, the United States began to expand. In 1803, it bought the Louisiana Territory from France, which doubled the size of the country. In 1819, it bought Florida from Spain. By the 1840s, Americans began to believe that it was their destiny to control most, if not all, of the North American continent. At the least, this meant expanding to the Pacific Ocean, and so the westward expansion continued.

President James Polk tried to buy California from Mexico, but Mexico refused to sell it. The Americans also wanted the Texas territory which belonged to Mexico. A number of Americans had settled there, and in 1845 the United States risked war with Mexico by taking the Texas territory. The following year there was a war—the Mexican-American War of 1846-1847. The Americans won, and, as a result, the United States kept Texas and gained more new territory—not only California, but all of what is now the southwestern part of the country.

---

[1] *a hemisphere*: Half of a sphere, here, the earth.

At the same time, after peaceful talks with Britain, the Oregon territory, which bordered on the Pacific Ocean, was added to the United States in 1846. The borders of the United States now reached from the Atlantic Ocean to the Pacific Ocean, and it was now a continental power.

Nearly fifty years passed before the United States seriously considered adding any more territory. The Americans were busy at home, with the fighting of the Civil War (1861-1865), the industrial revolution, the building of railroads, and the settling of the West. By the end of the nineteenth century, the United States had become a major economic power.

In 1898 the United States fought a short war with Spain—the Spanish-American War. It began as an idealistic effort to free Cuba from Spanish rule. A New York newspaper said that the aim of the war was "the liberty of human beings, for Cuba Libre, not for an extension of United States territory." But when the war ended, the United States took several Spanish territories: the Philippine Islands, Puerto Rico, and Guam. The United States began an experiment in imperialism. Most Americans believed that imperialism was wrong, and many protested against the imperialist expansion. They said that the United States had fought for its independence from the British empire, but now it was creating an empire of its own.

The United States kept the new territories. President McKinley did not know what he should do with them. He finally decided that it was America's responsibility to govern the Philippines, to educate the people, and to "civilize and Christianize" them. One historian has said that his philosophy was, "God directs us; perhaps it will pay."[2] After all, there would be new markets for American agricultural and industrial products, and also the islands would be useful as naval bases.

The United States experienced many difficulties in trying to control even a small empire. The experiment in imperialism was not generally seen as a success, and America did not try to add territories beyond its shores again.

---

[2]*perhaps it will pay*: perhaps it will be profitable

In the first decade of the twentieth century, the United States continued to steer clear of European political affairs. When World War I began in 1914, America declared that it would not enter the war. President Woodrow Wilson had strong pro-British[3] feelings, but he wanted to keep his country out of the war.

Eventually America entered the war, in 1917, as an ally of Britain, although there was still strong isolationist feeling in America. The Americans decided to enter the war because they were concerned about German submarine attacks on ships carrying American citizens.

After the war was over, President Wilson tried to change America's isolationist policies. He wanted the United States to become more involved in European affairs, and to join the new League of Nations. For the first time in their history, Americans were asked to enter an international organization, to take an active role in foreign affairs, and to try to help other nations keep peace in the world.

The United States Senate must approve all international treaties made by the government. The Senate refused to approve the treaty for the United States to join the League of Nations. President Wilson was extremely disappointed. He tried hard to persuade the American people that it was important to join the League of Nations, but he was not able to change the long policy of American isolationism.

The American preference for isolationism continued during the 1920s and 1930s. In the 1930s, Adolph Hitler rose to power in Germany. This worried President Franklin D. Roosevelt, but the majority of Americans still preferred noninvolvement in European affairs. In 1940, the British were alone in the efforts to stop Hitler. Roosevelt found it difficult to send help to Britain because there were strong isolationist forces in Congress. A bill to lend war equipment to Britain was defeated in the Senate. Isolationist Senator Taft said, "Lending war equipment is a good deal like[4] lending chewing gum. You don't want it back."

---

[3]*pro-British*: for the British
[4]*is a good deal like*: is very much like

On December 7, 1941, Japan (Germany's ally) attacked the American naval base at Pearl Harbor, Hawaii. Many American ships and planes were destroyed, and more than 3,000 Americans were killed. Now President Roosevelt had no trouble persuading Congress to declare war against Japan. Germany quickly declared war against the United States. The United States was involved in a second world war.

Most Americans expected foreign involvement to end after Germany and Japan were defeated in 1945, but this did not happen. The United States was now the most powerful nation in the world. It would have a new foreign policy and a new role in international affairs.

The United States and the Soviet Union were allies during World War II. President Roosevelt hoped that they could continue to cooperate after the war, and work together to build a lasting peace. He wanted the two countries to cooperate in a new international organization, the United Nations. Roosevelt died in the spring of 1945. The United Nations was established soon after his death, but his dream of Soviet-American cooperation did not come true.

The Soviet Union decided to keep its armies in Eastern Europe after the war to control the countries of Eastern Europe which it had defeated during the war. It supported communist parties there which would follow the wishes of the Soviet Union. Soviet control of Eastern Europe destroyed any hopes for cooperation between the United States and the Soviet Union.

When Roosevelt died in office in 1945, Harry S Truman became President. After the war ended, Truman decided that the spread of Soviet power had to be stopped before it reached Western Europe. Soviet power had to be "contained" by American action, and so President Truman created a policy of containment.

Truman's containment policy included both economic and military support for Western Europe. The United States had a plan to help the nations of Western Europe, which was called the Marshall Plan (after George C. Marshall, U.S. Secretary of State).[5] The Marshall Plan provided $17 billion to help

[5] *a Secretary of State*: An important official in the U.S. government.

Truman with Stalin and Atlee at the Berlin Conference, 1945
Library of Congress

Western Europe repair the terrible damage done by World War II. In five years, the nations of Western Europe were strong and independent again. The Marshall Plan was one of the greatest successes of Truman's containment policy.

In 1949, Truman added a military plan to his containment policy. The United States joined eleven other Western European and North American nations in a military alliance called NATO—the North Atlantic Treaty Organization. The NATO nations agreed that "an attack against one or more of them . . . shall be considered an attack against them all."

Originally, NATO and the Marshall Plan were created to contain, or check, Soviet power in Europe. Some of Truman's statements, however, suggested that the United States might go further, and try to expand this policy of containment around the world. The danger was that the United States might try to do too much. If it tried to police the entire world against communism, it would probably fail.

Truman understood this danger and tried to limit America's role as a world policeman. For example, he limited United States aid to Nationalist China. Nationalist China was threatened by the communist forces of Mao Tse Tung. Even when it seemed certain that Mao would gain control of mainland China, Truman did not send military aid. Then, in 1950, North Korea attacked South Korea. Truman believed it was necessary to give military aid to the South Koreans, calling it a "police action."

During the presidency of Dwight Eisenhower (1953-1961), the United States began to think of itself more and more as a world policeman. There was much concern over the spread of communism. Eisenhower's Secretary of State, John Foster Dulles, believed that communism threatened every area of the world. He believed the United States should risk even nuclear war to protect nations against communism.

John F. Kennedy became President in 1961. By that time, most Americans strongly believed that the United States should be a world policeman against communism. In his inauguration speech of 1961, Kennedy voiced this opinion. He declared, "Let every nation know . . . that we shall pay any price, . . . support any friend, oppose any foe[6] to assure the survival and the success of liberty."

Kennedy was assassinated in November, 1963. At that time, the United States had already become involved in Vietnam. Within a few years, the next President, Lyndon Johnson, greatly increased military aid to South Vietnam. The number of United States soldiers fighting there rose from about 16,000 to more than half a million.

After several years, Americans began to question their involvement in Vietnam. The protest movement grew, and there were large, sometimes violent, anti-war demonstrations. The American economy suffered. Finally, President Johnson decided not to send any more soldiers to Vietnam. Slowly and painfully the Americans ended their involvement in Vietnam. Many said it had been a mistake.

---

[6]*a foe*: an enemy

In the three decades from 1940 to 1970, American foreign policy had changed greatly. The United States had gone from one extreme position to another—from isolationism to world policeman. In the 1970s, Presidents Nixon, Ford and Carter tried to find a position between the two extremes. It is probable that future presidents will do the same.

NEW WORDS

communism   A form of government in which everything is owned by the people.

imperialism   A plan or policy of having an empire; having control over other nations or territories.

isolationism   Aloneness; a plan to stay separate from others.

to steer clear of   To avoid.

EXERCISES

Section One

A. Circle the letter next to the best answer.

1. George Washington, the first President of the United States, believed that the nation should
    a. make many alliances in order to protect itself.
    b. try to become involved in international politics.
    c. avoid alliances with foreign countries.

2. From 1801 until 1949, the United States
    a. had many alliances with countries such as France and Britain.
    b. had no alliances with any foreign countries.
    c. had a few alliances but did not become involved in any major wars during the 1800s.

3. The United States got California and what is now the southwestern part of the country
    a. by buying the territory from Mexico.
    b. after a war with Mexico.
    c. after peaceful talks with Britain.

4. After the U.S. had taken control of foreign territories in 1898,
   a. many Americans still believed it was wrong for the U.S. to have an empire.
   b. most Americans believed they should take control of many more countries.
   c. it returned the control to the natives of these countries immediately.

5. When World War I began in 1914,
   a. most Americans wanted to enter the war.
   b. the United States said it would not enter the war.
   c. President Woodrow Wilson wanted to enter the war, but Congress stopped him.

6. When World War I ended,
   a. the U.S. returned to its policy of noninvolvement in European affairs.
   b. the American public was eager to take an active role in foreign affairs.
   c. President Wilson refused to allow the U.S. to join the League of Nations.

7. In 1940, President Roosevelt
   a. was not worried about Hitler's rise to power.
   b. found it difficult to persuade the American public not to enter the war.
   c. found it difficult to persuade Congress to send help to Britain.

8. When Soviet armies remained in eastern European countries after World War II,
   a. the United States was happy to see them there.
   b. President Truman was not very concerned.
   c. President Truman believed the U.S. had to stop the spread of communism.

9. The Marshall Plan
   a. provided money to Western European countries to repair damage done by the war.
   b. was a military alliance between the U.S. and North America and Western Europe and North America.
   c. seemed like a good idea, but was really unsuccessful.

10. During the presidency of Dwight Eisenhower (1953-1961)
    a. the Americans began to think of the U.S. more and more as a "world policeman" against communism.
    b. there was not much concern in the United States about the spread of communism.
    c. the United States declared war on North Korea.

B. Circle the letter next to the best answer.

1. President Truman created a *policy* of containment after World War II.
   a. agreement
   b. plan
   c. treaty

2. George Washington advised his countrymen to *steer clear of* alliances with foreign countries.
   a. make
   b. avoid
   c. break

3. Such *alliances* might involve the United States in the wars of other countries.
   a. giving economic aid
   b. attacks on a foreign nation
   c. agreements to help another country

4. The United States established itself as a major power in the *Western Hemisphere.*
   a. Western Europe
   b. the area of foreign affairs
   c. North and South America

5. *Luckily for* the United States, Britain approved of the Monroe Doctrine.
   a. Britain was lucky.
   b. The United States was lucky.
   c. The Monroe Doctrine was lucky.

6. The United States began an experiment in *imperialism.*
   a. staying out of international politics.
   b. having an empire.
   c. steering clear of alliances.

7. Most Americans believed that what happened in Europe was not the *affair* of the United States.
   a. It was important to the Americans.
   b. What happened there mattered to the Americans.
   c. What happened there did not matter to the U.S.

8. President Wilson was *extremely* disappointed that the U.S. did not join the League of Nations.
   a. very
   b. a little
   c. eventually

9. President Roosevelt thought that the two nations would *cooperate*.
   a. They would be enemies.
   b. They would compete with each other.
   c. They would work together.

10. The United States offered *military* support to Western Europe.
    a. It sent money there to help repair the damage done by the war.
    b. It sent advisors there to help plan for a lasting peace.
    c. It send soldiers and equipment there to help protect the people.

C. Choose the word form which correctly completes each sentence. Put verbs into correct tenses. If necessary, make nouns plural.

   1. ally, alliance, to ally, allied
      a. The United States had no formal . . . . . . with foreign countries from 1801 to 1949.
      b. In 1949, the U.S. . . . . . . with Canada, Iceland and nine Western European countries to form NATO.
      c. The U.S. was considered one of the . . . . . . forces fighting Germany during World War I.
      d. Germany is now an . . . . . . of the United States.

   2. isolation, isolationism, to isolate, isolated
      a. The United States developed a policy of . . . . . . in order to avoid becoming involved in the wars of the great European powers.
      b. The U.S. tried . . . . . . itself from the rest of the world as much as possible.

    c. Because of its . . . . . . position an ocean away from Europe, it was possible to steer clear of involvement in European affairs.

    d. De Tocqueville described the geographical . . . . . . of the U.S. and the protection it provided the nation.

3.   expansion, expansionist, to expand

    a. In the early 1800s the U.S. began a time of great . . . .

    b. There have always been some Americans who wanted the U.S. . . . . . . beyond its shores.

    c. These . . . . . . wanted the U.S. to own territory outside its own continental borders.

4.   interference, to interfere

    a. The Monroe Doctrine of 1823 stated that European countries were not . . . . . . in the affairs of North and South American countries.

    b. In exchange, there would be no . . . . . . in European affairs by the Americans.

5.   imperialism, imperial, imperialist

    a. The people who were against . . . . . . believed that it was wrong for the United States to create an empire.

    b. . . . . . . nations are those which control nations outside their borders.

    c. Presidents Johnson and Nixon had such great power that some Americans referred to the . . . . . . presidency.

6.   preference, to prefer

    a. From the time of George Washington until after World War II, most Americans . . . . . . isolationism to involvement in international politics.

    b. The . . . . . for isolationism continued for two decades after World War I.

7.   containment, to contain

    a. President Truman created a policy of . . . . . . in order to stop the spread of Soviet power into Western Europe.

    b. His policy . . . . . . two types of aid—economic and military.

8.   extreme, extreme, extremely

    a. The United States has had two . . . . . . different foreign policies.

b. The two . . . . . . positions were isolationism and "world policeman."

c. In the three decades following World War II, the United States went from one . . . . . . to the other.

9. cooperation, to cooperate, cooperative

a. President Roosevelt hoped that the United States and the Soviet Union could continue . . . . . . after the war.

b. His dream of Soviet-American . . . . . . did not come true.

c. The United States had hoped that the Soviet Union would be more . . . .

10. communism, communist

a. The Soviet Union supported . . . . . . parties in Eastern European countries.

b. The United States was concerned about the spread of . . . . . . into Western Europe.

D. Rewrite each sentence. Choose one of these vocabulary words for the words and phrases in italics. Put verbs into the correct tense. If necessary, make nouns plural.

aid	imperialism
concern	isolationism
cooperate	major
expand	policy
extremely	steer clear of

1. Throughout most of their history, Americans have believed that they could and should avoid the responsibilities of an *important* world power.

2. If the new nation were to grow and develop, the United States would have to *avoid* involvement in foreign wars.

3. At the turn of the century, the United States began an experiment in *having control over foreign countries.*

4. In the 19th century, Americans were more *worried* about developing their own nation than they were about having a role in international politics.

5. After World War II, the United States had a new international role and it had to have a new *way of doing things.*

6. The U.S. policy of *staying separate* was not possible in the 1940s.

7. President Roosevelt had hoped that the U.S. and the Soviet Union could continue to *work together* after the war.

8. President Truman sent military and economic *help* to Western Europe after the war.

9. Truman's policy of containment was *made larger* to include other areas of the world.

10. Trying to be a world policeman against the spread of communism would be *very* difficult for any nation.

E. Use each group of words to make a sentence. Add other words, but use the words below in the form and order they are given.

1. role, United States, major power, recent one
2. Britain, ready, help, enforce, Monroe Doctrine
3. 1819, United States, bought, Florida, Spain
4. borders, United States, reached, Atlantic Ocean, Pacific Ocean
5. United States, had, opportunity, develop, empire
6. 1940, British, alone, efforts, stop, Hitler
7. United States, Soviet Union, allies, World War II
8. Marshall Plan, one, successes, Truman's, policy
9. Truman tried, limit, U.S., role, world policeman
10. 1970s, Presidents, tried, find, position, two extremes

F. The following paragraph is a summary of the chapter. Fill in the blanks with any word that makes sense.

The role of the _____ States as a major_____ power is a fairly_____ one. The first American_____ advised the new nation _____ avoid alliances with foreign_____. From around 1800 until _____World War II, the_____ had no foreign alliances._____ the 1800s the U.S._____ greatly. It added new_____ territories and established itself_____ a continental power. In_____ it gained control of _____territories after the Spanish-American_____. In the 20th century_____ preference for isolationism continued_____ after World War II._____1945 the foreign policy_____the U.S. began to_____. President Truman tried to _____the spread of communism. _____ U.S. gave economic aid_____

Western Europe and established_____ alliances. In the 1950s _____ 1960s, the United States _____ to play the role_____ "world policeman." Today_____ foreign policy is somewhere_____the extremes of isolationism_____ world policeman.

G. *Questions for Discussion and Composition.*

1. In the mid-1800s, many Americans believed it was their destiny to control most of the North American continent. Do you believe that a nation can have a "destiny"? If people believe their country has a special destiny, what effect does this belief have on their actions? What destiny do you believe your country has?

2. Discuss imperialism. Has your country ever had an empire? Has it ever been part of an empire belonging to a foreign nation? How do people in your country view imperialism?

3. Discuss the relationship between your country and the United States. Is there a formal alliance? If so, what does each nation agree to do for the other nation? Is there a military alliance? What kind of an economic relationship is there between the U.S. and your country? How do people in your country view the power of the U.S.?

4. Discuss the use of foreign aid. Do powerful nations have a responsibility to help other nations? What kind of help should they give? When should they provide economic support? When should they provide military aid? Which country should make these decisions—the country which gives aid, or the country which receives it?

5. Discuss the role of the United Nations. How is the United Nations viewed in your country? Does your country play an active role in the U.N.? What kind of power should the U.N. have? Should it be a "world policeman"?

6. Discuss the foreign policy of your country. What nations does it consider as friends? What nations does it consider as enemies? What formal alliances does your country have? How has its foreign policy changed since World War II?

Section Two

A. Fill in the blanks with *a, an* or *the* as needed. If no article is needed,
put an *X* in the blank.

In 1898 _____ United States fought _____ short war with _____
Spain, _____ Spanish-American War. It began as _____idealistic effort
to free_____ Cuba from _____ Spanish rule. _____ New York
newspaper said that _____ aim of _____ war was "_____liberty of
_____human beings, for_____ Cuba Libre, not for_____ extension of
_____ United States territory." But when _____ war ended, _____
United States took several _____ Spanish territories:_____ Philippine
Islands,_____ Puerto Rico, and _____ Guam. _____ United States
began _____experiment in_____imperialism.

B. Use the following words and phrases in sentences which clearly show
you understand their meaning.

1. to steer clear of
2. to be isolated from
3. to cooperate with (someone)
4. to come to the aid of
5. to have a preference for
6. to risk
7. to become involved in something (or with someone)
8. the Western Hemisphere
9. human beings
10. a treaty

C. *Chapter Outline: The Rise to World Power*[1]

I. Isolationism
   A. Policy against foreign alliances
   B. Monroe Doctrine

II. Growth of the U.S.
    A. Expansion of continental U.S.
    B. Addition of foreign territories

III. Involvement in world wars
     A. World War I
     B. World War II

[1]See Introduction, page vii, for suggested ways to use this chapter
outline.

IV. Role as major world power (after World War II)
    A. Policy of containment
    B. Role as world policeman

D. Expand the chapter outline in C above by adding supporting details. Skim the chapter to find the information. For example, the supporting details for the first part are found in the first four paragraphs of the chapter.

    You may have as many details for each point as you wish. Number them 1, 2, 3, etc. If you have further details, letter them a, b, c, etc. Expand all four parts of the outline in this way.

E. There are several ways to organize the information in this chapter, since it is not divided into clear sections. The information is arranged in chronological order; that is, the events are arranged in the order in which they happened. The chapter begins with the foreign policy of the first U.S. President, and ends with the foreign policy of the present time.

    One way to outline the chapter, then, would be to divide it into periods or divisions of time. The historical events would be arranged under divisions of time such as the nineteenth century and the twentieth century.

    Another way to outline the chapter would be by ideas. For example, the chapter begins by explaining the policy of isolationism. Since this policy continued in one form or another until after World War II, isolationism is mentioned throughout the chapter. It would be possible to make an outline of isolationism alone.

    Choose one of the subjects listed below and write an outline of the information found in the chapter on that subject. You may do either a *topic* outline or a *sentence* outline. Skim the chapter to find the information you need.

1. Isolationism
2. Nineteenth century foreign policy
3. Twentieth century foreign policy
4. Wars with other nations
5. U.S. relations with Britain
6. The United States and communism
7. The role of U.S. Presidents in shaping foreign policy

F. Write a composition following the outline you wrote in exercise E.

Main Street USA

Boys with Lincoln

A farmer

Mike Morse

CHAPTER 8

THE AMERICAN CHARACTER

Do not trouble yourself much to get new things. . . . Sell your clothes and keep your thoughts.

Henry David Thoreau
(writer) 1854

I say that you ought to get rich, and it is your duty to get rich.

Russell H. Conwell
(Protestant preacher) 1861

What do Americans believe in? What is the American character? These questions are hard to answer, because there are so many Americans and they believe in so many different things. However, the history of the United States does provide some understanding of certain basic characteristics that many Americans share.

One of the main reasons why the early settlers came to America was to escape the controls they had experienced in Europe. There, small groups of wealthy people prevented them

135

from moving into a higher social position or becoming wealthy, and government-supported churches controlled their religious practices and beliefs. Because these early settlers wanted to be free from such controls, they brought to America the view that the individual was supremely important. The settlers were against the efforts of the church, the society, and particularly the government, to control their actions. These controls came to be viewed as "un-American."

This strong American belief in individualism has both positive and negative sides. On the positive side, it has strengthened Americans' inventiveness and their belief in hard work. On the negative side, the belief in individualism has sometimes prevented Americans from using their government to solve their common problems. Americans prefer not to have government solutions to social problems.

The belief in individualism is a basic part of the American character. This belief has at least two separate parts—idealism and materialism. Although these two beliefs are quite different, most Americans try to live with them both at the same time, and idealism and materialism are both very much a part of the American character.

American idealism comes largely from the nation's Protestant religious heritage. Because many of the early settlers came to America seeking religious freedom, religion played an important role in their lives. Morality was an important concern, and there was a strong belief in the moral responsibility of the individual. Early Americans did not have to belong to any particular church to have this belief. It influenced all Americans so strongly that idealism came to mean that each individual should possess a high moral character, and should live by his or her own beliefs. This is what American idealism means today.

Americans also have a strong belief in materialism, that is, that each individual should gain as much wealth as possible. The American belief in materialism is partly a result of the nation's great material abundance. The early settlers found a continent with great forests, rivers, and fertile farmland in abundance. It is not surprising that many viewed America as the land of opportunity.

As the United States grew and developed, the supply of natural resources seemed endless, and so did the opportunities for personal economic advancement. Each generation had a chance to become wealthier than their parents had been. Generation after generation of new immigrants had the same opportunity. Americans eventually developed the belief that it was almost a duty to get rich. Men like Russell Conwell said it was their "Christian and godly duty to do so."

American history provides many examples of the philosophy of both idealism and materialism. An excellent example of American idealism is the writer Henry David Thoreau (1817-1862). Thoreau was strongly opposed to materialism in American life. He was a supreme idealist, whose main concern was the perfection of the individual. Although he personally disliked organized religion, he often read the Bible[1] and he respected its teachings.

Thoreau believed very strongly in the individual conscience. He believed that a person should make decisions on the basis of his or her conscience, and that an individual should refuse to obey a law that he or she did not believe was right. Thoreau himself was arrested in 1846 for doing this. He refused to pay his taxes because he was opposed to the Mexican-American War. He believed that the United States would annex[2] Texas if it won the war, and that slavery would be permitted in Texas. Thoreau was opposed to slavery, and he refused to support a war which would increase the practice of slavery. He was arrested and spent one night in prison. The next day some of his friends paid his tax for him and he went home.

Thoreau's idealism led him to criticize other areas of American life. He criticized materialistic individualism which values wealth more than beauty. He complained that if a man spends a day in the woods because he loves their beauty, he is called lazy. But if a man spends the day there cutting down all the trees to sell them and make money, he is called a hard-working citizen.

Thoreau was not a typical American because he did not believe in idealism and materialism at the same time; he

[1]*the Bible*: The book of the Christian religion
[2]*to annex*: To add to one's own property

represents only the idealistic side of the American character. Thoreau has continued to interest millions of Americans. Martin Luther King, Jr., the civil rights leader, studied the writings of Thoreau. King himself refused to obey segregation laws which he believed were unjust, and he went to prison. So did many college-age students who were strongly opposed to the United States' involvement in the Vietnam war. Many of these students were influenced by Thoreau's writings.

Just as there are examples of pure idealism, so there are examples of pure materialism. The materialistic side of the American character can be seen in men like Jim Fisk, one of the railroad owners of the late 1800s. Ideals and morals meant nothing to him. He was only interested in money and power.

In his fight to gain control of the railroads, Fisk often broke the law. He and his business friends sold stock[3] illegally, refused to obey court orders, and made payments to legislators and government officials who would help them. Fisk was often in trouble with the law. Once, when the New York state police were chasing him, he and his friends escaped by crossing the state line into New Jersey. The New York police chased them to the border, but had no power to arrest them in another state. Safe in New Jersey, Fisk was proud of his escape from the police. He told newsmen, "As ambitious young men, we saw there was no chance for us there to expand, and so we came over here to grow up with the country . . ."

Like most Americans, Fisk believed in taking full advantage of the nation's great abundance to gain wealth. Yet Jim Fisk is not usually given a place of respect in American history books. His materialism was too extreme. Most Americans want both ideals and material wealth. They live with a compromise between the two: one must have a high moral character, but this must not interfere with enjoying a high standard of living, and vice versa.

Americans seem to respect leaders who understand this compromise. The presidents who have earned the lasting

---

[3]*stock*: The shares of a business, which are bought and owned by individuals.

respect of the American people have succeeded partly because they have based their actions on ideas acceptable to both sides of the American character.

Abraham Lincoln faced the problem of slavery in this way. He welcomed the support of those who opposed slavery for moral reasons, but he also knew that he needed the support of those who opposed slavery for economic reasons. Some of the northern farmers wanted to move into the new western territories and they did not want to compete with farmers who used slave labor, which made their costs lower. They therefore opposed the spread of slavery into the new western territories. In presenting his anti-slavery views to the public, Lincoln was able to unite those in the North who opposed slavery for idealistic reasons with those who opposed it for materialistic reasons.

In the past, there have been many disagreements about the roles of idealism and materialism in American life. These disagreements have been in many areas—foreign policy, economics, government regulation of business, civil rights. For two centuries the Americans' belief in materialism was supported by abundant resources. It was not until the late 1960s and the 1970s that Americans began to see any limits. Then the war in Vietnam and the energy problems caused them to see limits. Americans have had to face the prospect of less abundance. For the first time they face the prospect of a new generation having less material wealth than the last one. Perhaps hardest of all, they face changes in their own standard of living in the future.

Perhaps the idealistic side of their character will help Americans find solutions to some of their problems. President Kennedy said in his inauguration speech in 1961, "Ask not what your country can do for you—ask what you can do for your country." He was speaking to the idealism of the American people.

The debate between idealism and materialism is likely to continue in the United States. The positive and negative characteristics of each will be discussed, as they have been for years. There has been far less debate on the value of individualism, however. Most Americans believe that the individual and his or her rights are the foundation of their democracy. The belief in individualism is perhaps the strongest and most basic belief Americans have.

The idealist Henry David Thoreau and the materialist Jim Fisk seem to be completely different types of men, yet they shared a belief in the importance of the individual. They both believed that the individual, free of controls, creates what is good in human society. They also believed that government, even democratic government, is a bad thing.

American individualism has encouraged freedom, hard work, and inventiveness throughout the history of the United States, but it has created weaknesses as well as strengths. Individualism has not encouraged Americans to save the natural resources of their land, and there has been much waste of land, energy, and other resources. Americans like to live in individual houses and drive individual cars. Their standard of living has been based on abundant resources. As resources become less abundant, the government may have to pass laws to stop individuals from being so wasteful.

Individualism has not encouraged Americans to plan for their common future. Many of the problems in the future will probably need national solutions—pollution control, energy management, and mass transportation[4] systems, for example. Most Americans would probably agree with Thoreau, "That government is best which governs least." But whether they like it or not, Americans can probably expect their government to play a larger role in their lives in the future. They must use their elected governments to plan for the future. If they plan wisely, perhaps the United States will continue to be a nation where individuals have the right to "life, liberty, and the pursuit of happiness."

---

[4]*mass transportation*: A way to move a large number of people at one time, e.g., by bus, train, or plane, rather than by the use of individual vehicles.

NEW WORDS

abundance Richness, great plenty.

to face the prospect To think about the possibility of something happening in the future; to face a problem and try to solve it.

materialism A love of material wealth; a love of things.

morality Doing what is right.

a standard of living The material level at which a person lives; a rich person is said to have a high standard of living.

EXERCISES

Section One

A. Circle the letter next to the best answer.

1. The early settlers who came to America
   a. wanted to have their government control the activities of the churches.
   b. wanted to be free from the controls of the churches, the society and the government.
   c. believed that the wishes and the welfare of the society were more important than those of the individual.

2. The strong belief in individualism
   a. has encouraged Americans to invent new things.
   b. has discouraged them from working hard.
   c. has encouraged them to use their government to find solutions to national problems.

3. American idealism
   a. comes from the fact that the American land had great natural resources.
   b. was a popular idea among members of particular churches.
   c. means that each individual should have a good moral character.

4. Henry David Thoreau
   a. did not believe in government at all, refused to obey laws, and spent much time in prison.
   b. believed that a person should decide what to do on the basis of his or her individual moral conscience.
   c. believed in the value of hard work and felt it was more important than valuing beauty.

5. Most Americans
   a. believe that ideals are more important than material possessions.
   b. believe that material possessions are more important than ideals.
   c. want both moral ideals and material wealth.

6. The American belief in materialism
   a. has been supported by abundant resources for over two centuries.
   b. has had no effect on areas such as foreign policy, economics, government regulation of business, etc.
   c. has interfered with the wish to have a high standard of living.

7. In the late 1960s and 1970s
   a. nothing happened to change the view that American resources were limitless.
   b. the war in Vietnam and the energy problems caused the Americans to see limits to their resources.
   c. Americans had no reason to believe that the next generation could not be wealthier than the present one.

8. There has always been little debate in America
   a. on the value of individualism.
   b. on the value of idealism.
   c. on the value of materialism.

9. Most Americans believe that
   a. the individual and his rights are the foundation of their democracy.
   b. the United States must have a strong government to stop individuals from doing the wrong thing.
   c. it is good to have the government play an important role in their lives.

10. When President Kennedy said, "Ask not what your country can do for you—ask what you can do for your country," he was encouraging people to be
    a. individualistic.
    b. materialistic.
    c. idealistic.

B. Circle the letter next to the best answer.

1. This strong belief in individualism has both *positive* and *negative* sides.
    a. Some people are for it and some are against it.
    b. It is a strong belief because people consider both sides important.
    c. The belief is good in some ways and bad in others.

2. The belief in individualism has two separate parts—idealism and *materialism.*
    a. the belief that a person's moral character should determine his or her actions
    b. the belief that each person should gain as much wealth and as many things as possible
    c. the belief that the individual has the right to own property without interference from the government

3. The American religious heritage speaks of *morality.*
    a. the church
    b. working hard
    c. doing what is right

4. The American belief in materialism is probably a result of the nation's great material *abundance.*
    a. richness or plenty
    b. strength
    c. opportunities

5. *Generation* after generation of new immigrants had the chance to become wealthy.
    a. People coming from different countries all had the same opportunity to become wealthy.
    b. The opportunity for children to become wealthier than their parents continued for many, many years.
    c. People whose culture and religion were different all had the chance to become wealthy.

6. Thoreau was strongly *opposed* to materialism in American life.
    a. He was in favor of it; he thought it was good.
    b. He believed it should be part of American life.
    c. He was against it; he thought it was bad.

7. Americans want to have a high *standard of living.*
    a. They want to have a high moral character.
    b. They want good jobs, houses, cars, clothing, food and other things.
    c. They want to be good people and do the right thing.

8. Americans have had to *face the prospect* of less abundance.
    a. There is less abundance in America now.
    b. They have had to think about the possibility of having less abundance in the future.
    c. They have avoided thinking about having less abundance in the future.

9. The positive and negative characteristics of each will be *debated.*
    a. People will choose the good and not the bad.
    b. The positive and negative characteristics are equal.
    c. The characteristics of each will be discussed.

10. Many of the problems in the future will probably need national solutions—pollution control, energy management, and *mass transportation* systems, for example.
    a. moving large numbers of people from place to place at one time
    b. finding large numbers of people places to live
    c. finding good jobs for large numbers of people

C. Choose the word form which correctly completes each sentence. Put verbs into the correct tense. If necessary, make nouns plural.

1. character, characteristic, to characterize, characteristic, characteristically
   a. Idealism and materialism are both very much a part of the American . . . .
   b. Rugged individualism is a . . . . . . which is admired by most Americans.
   c. It is difficult to . . . . . . the beliefs of the typical American.
   d. Americans are . . . . . . independent, resourceful, and practical.
   e. What qualities are . . . . . . of people in your country?

2. material, materialism, materialistic
   a. Americans are often criticized for being too . . . .
   b. The American belief in . . . . . . is probably a result of the nation's abundant resources.
   c. The British were eager to establish colonies as centers of trade so that they could get the many raw . . . . . . of North America for use in their factories.

3. moral, morality, to moralize, moral, morally
   a. The Protestant religious heritage speaks of . . . .
   b. It is a belief in the . . . . . . responsibility of the individual.
   c. The individual is . . . . . . responsible to God for his actions.
   d. Most Americans believe that people should have high . . . .
   e. Some religious leaders try to . . . . . . about various areas of American life.

4. abundance, to abound, abundant, abundantly
   a. The early settlers found a continent with . . . . . . natural resources.
   b. Forests, rivers and fertile farmland . . . .
   c. Americans have believed, until recently, that there was no limit to this . . . .
   d. It is becoming . . . . . . clear, however, that America's resources are not limitless.

5. opposition, to oppose, opposite
   a. Thoreau strongly . . . . . . the Mexican-American War.

b. His . . . . . . was based on the fact that if the U.S. won the war, it would take Texas and make it a slave state.

c. Thoreau believed that ideals were more important than material possessions; Fisk had the . . . . . . view.

6. face, to face
   a. Thoreau decided he . . . . . . going to prison, rather than paying taxes to support a war he did not believe in.
   b. Civil rights leaders came . . . . . . to . . . . . . with policemen during the demonstrations in the South.

7. debate, to debate, debatable
   a. The roles of idealism and materialism in the American society are often . . . .
   b. This . . . . . . between idealists and materialists has continued for generations.
   c. Whether the questions can ever be answered is . . . .

8. type, to typify, typical, typically
   a. It is difficult to describe the . . . . . . person of any nationality.
   b. There are so many . . . . . . of behavior to describe.
   c. What characteristics do you believe . . . . . . Americans?
   d. Are people in your country . . . . . . independent and individualistic?

9. invention, inventor, inventiveness, to invent, inventive
   a. An . . . . . . is a person who . . . . . . something new.
   b. The belief in individualism has strengthened American . . . .
   c. Thomas Edison is an American who is famous for his many . . . .
   d. Benjamin Franklin, one of the founding fathers, was an . . . . . . person.

10. value, to value, valuable
    a. Most Americans . . . . . . moral ideals.
    b. A good moral character is a . . . . . . quality.
    c. There is also a strong belief in the . . . . . . of the individual and his rights.

D. Choose the word which correctly completes the sentence.

1. Abraham Lincoln had to (face—avoid) the problem of slavery in America.

2. Thoreau believed that a person should (obey—disobey) a law which went against his or her conscience.

3. Martin Luther King, Jr., refused to obey segregation laws which he believed were (just—unjust).

4. The idealists (opposed—supported) slavery because they believed it was morally wrong.

5. There is much (agreement—disagreement) over the value of materialism in the American society.

6. Inventiveness is a (positive—negative) quality.

7. Jim Fisk was a very (moral—immoral) man, who did many illegal things.

8. Americans now realize that the energy resources of their country are (limited—limitless).

9. The energy problems facing the world are (escapable—inescapable).

10. Oil and coal are still (valuable—worthless) natural resources.

E. Fill in the blanks with *the, a* or *an.* If none are needed, write an *X* in the blank.

In_____ past, there have been many disagreements about _____roles of _____ idealism and _____ materialism in _____American life. These disagreements have been in_____ many areas— _____ foreign policy, _____ economics, _____government regulation of _____ business, _____civil rights. For_____ two centuries_____ Americans' belief in _____materialism was supported by _____ abundant resources. It was not until_____late 1960s and_____1970s that Americans began to see any limits. Then_____war in _____ Vietnam and _____ energy problems caused them to see limits. Americans have had to face _____ prospect of_____ less abundance. For _____first time they have had to face_____ prospect of_____ new generation having_____less material wealth than_____ last one. Perhaps hardest of all, they face _____ changes in their own standard of _____living in _____future.

F. Use each group of words to make a sentence. Add other words, but use the words below in the form and order they are given.

1. settlers, came, continent, reasons
2. belief, individualism, has, positive, negative, sides
3. idealism, materialism, both, part, American character
4. Thoreau, opposed, materialism, American life
5. Thoreau, refused, pay, taxes, because, opposed, Mexican-American War
6. Thoreau, not, typical American
7. Americans, live, compromise, idealism, materialism
8. Americans, have had, face, prospect, less abundance
9. debate, idealism, materialism, likely, continue, U.S.
10. Americans, can expect, government, play, larger role, lives, future

G. The following paragraph is a summary of the chapter. Fill in the blanks with any word that makes sense.

Americans have a strong _____ in individualism. This belief _____ both positive and negative _____. It has at least _____ parts—idealism and materialism. _____ idealism comes from the _____ Protestant religious heritage. It _____ a belief that each _____ should possess a high _____ character. American materialism comes _____ the nation's great material _____. It is the belief _____ each individual should gain _____ much wealth as he _____ . Thoreau is an example _____ the philosophy of idealism. _____ is an example of _____ philosophy of materialism. Most _____ want both moral ideals _____ material wealth. They live _____ a compromise between idealism _____ materialism. Their belief in _____ is their strongest and _____ basic belief. Most Americans _____ that the individual and _____ rights are the foundation _____ their democracy.

H. *Questions for Discussion and Composition.*

1. Discuss individualism. Does the idea of "rugged individualism" exist in your country? How important are the rights of individuals in your country? Is the individual more important than society? How can people have individual freedom and still live together peacefully in a society?

2. What kinds of controls over individuals are there in your country? How much power and influence does the church have? How much control do the wealthy people of high social position have? What things does your government do to control individuals?

3. Discuss idealism. What does idealism mean in your country? Name a famous person in your country who is considered to be an idealist. What does he or she believe? What has this person done? How are idealists viewed in your country?

4. Discuss materialism. What does a materialistic person believe? How does a materialistic person act? How is materialism viewed in your country? What material things do most people in your country want? How important are material possessions such as cars?

5. How can a person, or a nation, be both idealistic and materialistic? Are people in your country more idealistic, or materialistic? Are women more idealistic than men? Are women more materialistic than men? How would you describe yourself? If you had a million dollars, how would you spend it?

6. Thoreau believed in "civil disobedience"—not obeying laws which are unjust. How important do you think an individual's conscience is? Has anyone in your country practiced "civil disobedience"? If so, what happened? Would you ever consider not obeying a law you believed was unjust?

Section Two

A. Write capital letters, commas, periods, and parentheses where they are needed.

american history provides many examples of the philosophy of both idealism and materialism an excellent example of american idealism is the writer henry david thoreau 1817-1862 thoreau was strongly opposed to materialism in american life he was a supreme idealist whose main concern was the perfection of the individual although he personally disliked organized religion he often read the bible and he respected its teachings

B. Use these words and phrases in sentences that clearly show you understand their meaning.

1. characteristics
2. materialistic
3. abundant
4. generation
5. to oppose
6. standard of living
7. to face the prospect of
8. to debate
9. typical
10. to be for (or against) something

C.   *Chapter Outline: The American Character*[1]

I.   Individualism
      A. Origin
      B. Definition
      C. Positive and negative sides

II.   Idealism
      A. Origin
      B. Definition

III. Materialism
      A. Origin
      B. Definition

IV.   Examples of two philosophies (idealism and materialism)
      A. Idealist—Henry David Thoreau
          1. Beliefs
          2. Actions
      B. Materialist—Jim Fisk
          1. Beliefs
          2. Actions

V.   The American compromise between idealism and materialism
      A. Definition
      B. Example—Abraham Lincoln and slavery
      C. Debate in American society

---

[1]See Introduction, page vii, for suggested ways to use this chapter outline.

VI. Conclusion—individualism
   A. Importance
   B. Weaknesses

D. The chapter outline in C above tells the kind of information given in the chapter, but it does not give the information itself. Skim the chapter, find the information, and rewrite the outline. You may wish to write your outline in sentence form. For example:

I. The Americans have a strong belief in individualism.
   A. The early settlers came to America to escape controls over the individual.
   B. The settlers believed that the individual was supremely important.
   C. The belief in individualism has both positive and negative sides.
      1. On the positive side, it has encouraged Americans to be inventive and to work hard.
      2. On the negative side, it has discouraged Americans from using their government to solve problems in their society.

E. Write an outline for a composition on American idealism, materialism, or individualism. Use information found in this chapter and add ideas of your own. When you have completed your outline, write a composition following the outline.

F. Read the following paragraph about Andrew Carnegie. How does he illustrate the American compromise between idealism and materialism? Write an outline and then a composition on this subject.

Andrew Carnegie was born in Scotland and came to the United States as a poor immigrant. He built an empire in the steel industry and became one of the richest men in the world. He liked to philosophize about his experience in America and wrote a book called *The Gospel of Wealth.* Carnegie believed that every person has the God-given right and duty to become as rich as possible. He believed that individuals should share their wealth, but only if they freely choose to. In 1900, Carnegie sold his businesses to the banker J.P. Morgan for $400 million. He spent the rest of his life using his money to help others. Carnegie built over 2,500 free public libraries at a cost of $56 million. By the time he died, Andrew Carnegie had given away more than $308 million.

Answers to the exercises

CHAPTER ONE

Section One

A. 1a, 2c, 3b, 4c, 5a, 6b, 7a, 8b, 9b, 10b
B. 1c, 2a, 3b, 4a, 5c, 6c, 7b, 8c, 9a, 10b
C. 1a historian, b historical, c history, d Historically; 2a to settle, b settlers, c settlement, d settled; 3a regional, b region, c regionalism; 4a urban, b urbanized, c Urbanization; 5a to pollute, b pollution, c polluted; 6a located, b location; 7a varies, b variety, c various; 8a industrialize, b Industrialization, industries, c industrial; 9a criticized, b critical, c critically, d criticism; 10a equal, b equality, c equally, d equals
D. *Possible answers*: 1. More and more people came to settle the land. 2. The fertile land of the north-central plains is excellent for farming. 3. On the other side of the Rockies is the Pacific Coast. 4. In 1849, gold was discovered in California. 5. The climate of the continental United States is varied. 6. The Northeast is the oldest region in the United States. 7. The settlement of the Northeast began in 1620 in Massachusetts. 8. Detroit is the center of the car industry. 9. The West was the last region to be settled. 10. One out of every ten Americans lives in the state of California.
E. *Possible answers*: given, There, land, came, The, Atlantic, the, fertile, River, Plains, Mountains, stretches, to, United, the, the, are, Alaska, four, the, the, of, open, are, land, Americans, their

Section Two

A. X, the, X, the, X, X, a, the, a, X, an, a, the, X, X, X, X, X, the, the, X, X (*or* the), the, the, X, the, X
B. See page 4.

CHAPTER TWO

Section One

A. 1b, 2b, 3b, 4c, 5a, 6a, 7b, 8b, 9b, 10b
B. 1c, 2a, 3c, 4a, 5c, 6a, 7a, 8b, 9c, 10b
C. 1a immigrated, b immigration, c immigrants; 2a colonies, b colonize, c colonists, d colonial; 3a were established, b establishment,

c established; 4a similarities, b similar, c similarly; 5a culturally,
b cultural, c culture; 6a reservations, b were reserved; 7a ancestral,
b ancestors, c ancestry; 8a races, b racially, c racial; 9a nationalities, b nation, c national, d nationally; 10a slavery, b slaves,
c was enslaved

D.   1. immigrants, 2. permanent, 3. heritage, 4. institutions, similar,
5. culture, 6. natives, 7. tribes, 8. reservations, 9. slaves, 10. taken a
more active role in

E.   *Possible answers:* 1. Some colonies were established as centers of
trade. 2. The beliefs of the Puritans are a part of the American
heritage. 3. This common language has been a tie between the two
nations. 4. Many Africans were brought to America to be sold as
slaves. 5. These immigrants caused many changes in American
society.

F.   *Possible answers:* of, to, immigrants, North, The, number, the,
early, the, American, by, Indians, on, brought, as, War, United,
numbers, and, and, their, the, 1900s, arrived, many, has, out, has

Section Two

A.   See page 26.

CHAPTER THREE

Section One

A.   1b, 2c, 3b, 4c, 5b, 6a, 7a, 8b, 9a, 10b
B.   1b, 2c, 3a, 4b, 5a, 6c, 7a, 8c, 9a, 10b
C.   1a Revolutionary, b revolted, c Revolution; 2a depended, b independent, c independently, independence; 3a to tax, b taxation,
c taxable, d tax; 4a legislature, b legislative, c legislators, d legislation, e to legislate; 5a to protest, b protestors, c protest; 6a pursuit,
b pursue; 7a to declare, b declaration; 8a philosophers, b philosophy, c philosophical, d philosophize, e Philosophically; 9a founding, b foundation, c was founded, d founders; 10a hero, b heroic,
c heroically, d heroism

D.   1. taxes, 2. legislature, 3. representatives, 4. protest, 5. weapons,
6. the situation, 7. independent, 8. documents, 9. found, 10. involved

E.   *Possible answers:* colonies, Great, reasons, their, reason, Americans,
be, British, Americans, the, governing, British, their, most, eventually, Americans, British, they, tax, said, that, to, became, for

Section Two

A.   1. Jefferson was a political philosopher. 2. George Washington was
from Virginia. 3. During the War against the French and Indians
(1754-1763), Britain had sent many soldiers to protect the
colonists. 4. The colonists did not like the new British taxes.
5. Soon after the fighting began, a group of colonial leaders met to
discuss the situation.

C.   *Possible answers*: 1. The American colonies decided to establish an
independent nation. 2. The colonists did not like the new taxes.
3. A group of leaders met to discuss the situation. 4. People have
the right to change their government. 5. The founding fathers
helped to found the new nation. 6. It caused a number of colonists
to leave the country. 7. Washington was a hero of the Revolutionary War. 8. The War of Independence caused hatred between
the British and the Americans. 9. Many Americans continued to
view Britain as the enemy of freedom. 10. The memories of war
continued for many years.

E.   I.   The events leading to the war
        A. The British taxation of the colonies in the 1760s
        B. The colonists' protests against taxation
      II.   The beginning of the fighting
        A. The meeting of the Continental Congress
        B. The decision to declare independence
          1. Thomas Jefferson and the Declaration of Independence
      III. The fighting of the war
        A. The leadership of George Washington
          1. Leader of the poorly armed American army
        B. The effects of the war
          1. The hatred between the British and the Americans

CHAPTER FOUR

Section One

A.   1a, 2a, 3b, 4b, 5c, 6b, 7b, 8c, 9b, 10b
B.   1b, 2b, 3c, 4a, 5c, 6b, 7c, 8b, 9c, 10c
C.   1a Constitution, b constitutionality, c constitutional; 2a supreme,
b supremacy, c supremely; 3a system, b systematically, c systematic; 4a check, b checks; 5a impeachment, b impeaches, c impeachable; 6a to amend, b amendments; 7a democracy, b democratic,

democratically; 8a presidential, b President, c presides, d presidency; 9a union, b united, c unity; 10a elected, b election, c electors, d electoral, e elected

D. 1. Constitution, 2. system, 3. executive branch, 4. judicial branch, 5. signs, bill, 6. veto, 7. term, 8. serve, 9. amendments, 10. provide

E. See page 59.

F. *Possible answers*: of, to, The, new, national, the, of, separated, three, This, checks, branches, legislative, Congress, the, led, The, feared, want, too, provided, changing, amendments, of, a, had, have, develop

Section Two

A. *Possible answers*: 1. A number of the leaders agreed that the nation needed a stronger government. 2. In 1787 they decided to meet in Philadelphia. 3. The Constitution created a completely new system of government. 4. There would be a system of checks and balances in the government. 5. The Constitution divides the government of the United States into three branches. 6. Congress is divided into two houses. 7. The President is the leader of the executive branch of the government. 8. The President signs his name on each piece of legislation. 9. Congress has the power to pass laws. 10. The third branch of the national government is the judicial branch.

B. X, X, the, the, The, the, X, X, The, X, a, X, the, the, the, X, X, X, X, X, the, the, X, X, the, X

CHAPTER FIVE

Section One

A. 1c, 2b, 3a, 4a, 5c, 6c, 7a, 8c, 9a, 10b

B. 1c, 2c, 3a, 4c, 5a, 6c, 7c, 8b, 9c, 10b

C. 1a encouraged, b encouraging, c encouragement, d encouragingly; 2a contradictory, b contradiction, c contradicted; 3a were freed, b freedmen, c freedom, d free; 4a segregation, b to segregate, c segregated; 5a integrated, b to integrate, c Integration; 6a compromise, b compromises; 7a temporary, b temporarily; 8a demonstrations, b demonstrators, c demonstrated; 9a discriminating, b discrimination; 10a legal, b legally, c was legalized

D. 1. temporary, 2. inequality, 3. minority, 4. freedmen, 5. illegal, 6. encouraged, 7. uncivilized, 8. segregation, 9. inexpensively, 10. descendants

E. 1. to, 2. by, 3. for, 4. of, 5. to, 6. by, 7. to, for, 8. for, of, to, to, of, 9. for, 10. for

F. *Possible answers*: Independence, there, between, and, living, Most, Slavery, in, it, and, until, Civil, War, in, South, against, laws, Blacks', groups, for, want, themselves, and

Section Two

A. *Possible answers*: 1. The first slaves were brought to North America in 1619. 2. Blacks were denied many opportunities which Whites had. 3. Slavery in a free society is a contradiction. 4. Crops were harvested by slaves in the South. 5. King led non-violent demonstrations against segregation. 6. Policemen tried to stop the demonstrators with fire hoses. 7. Dubois believed that integration was necessary. 8. The slaves were freed by the Thirteenth Amendment to the Constitution. 9. The modern civil rights movement began a decade after World War II. 10. The Puerto Ricans have demanded the use of Spanish as well as English in the public schools.

CHAPTER SIX

Section One

A. 1b, 2c, 3b, 4b, 5a, 6b, 7b, 8c, 9c, 10b

B. 1a, 2c, 3a, 4a, 5a, 6b, 7a, 8c, 9a, 10b

C. 1a agricultural, b agriculture, c agriculturally; 2a based, b basement, c basically, d basis, e basic; 3a economics, economist, b economy, c economic, d economically, e economical, f to economize; 4a individualism, b individuals, c individually, individualize, individual; 5a equipped, b to equip, c equipment; 6a monopolizing, b monopoly; 7a reform, b reformers, c reform; 8a to regulate, b regulation, c regularly, d regular; 9a depression, b were depressed, c depressed, d depressing; 10a retire, b retired, c retirement

D. 1. an agricultural, 2. economy, 3. rugged, 4. villains, 5. monopolies, 6. labor, 7. support, 8. reform, 9. regulate, 10. retire

E. See page 101.

F. *Possible answers*: 1. Rockefeller built an empire in the area of oil refining. 2. Many of the leaders of business were cruel men. 3. The businessmen were heroes in the eyes of some Americans. 4. Powerful reform movements were organized in the South, West, and Midwest. 5. In the 1890s millions of farmers were organized. 6. The factory workers in the cities were suffering. 7. The government began to regulate businesses more closely. 8. These Presidents seemed to be listening to the voice of the people. 9. People believed that the individual did not need help from the government. 10. Most Americans do not want to destroy the welfare system.

G. *Possible answers:* the, an, industrial, businessmen, very, steel, banks, businessmen, because, farmers, protest, workers, bargained, supported, the, business, the, bad, created, provide, Americans, business

Section Two

B. as, In, to, as, of, As, in, in, to, on, of, in, of, of, on, to

D. I. A. 1. The defeat of the South in the Civil War
2. The new power of the North after the Civil War
B. 1. The rich and powerful railroad owners
2. Other rich and powerful businessmen
C. 1. The American belief in economic opportunity
2. The American belief in rugged individualism
II. A. 1. The protest against high prices and business monopolies
2. The organization of political protest parties
B. 1. The protest against low pay and poor working conditions
2. The organization of labor unions
C. 1. The leadership of Presidents Theodore Roosevelt and Woodrow Wilson
2. The passing of new laws to regulate business activity
III. A. 1. The need for jobs and money for the unemployed
2. The need for payments to retired workers
B. 1. The new government programs established by President Franklin Roosevelt
2. The creation of the welfare state
C. 1. The Americans' criticism of big government and the welfare state
2. The Americans' belief that government (and business) should serve the people's needs

CHAPTER SEVEN

Section One

A. 1c, 2b, 3b, 4a, 5b, 6a, 7c, 8c, 9a, 10a

B. 1b, 2b, 3c, 4c, 5b, 6b, 7c, 8a, 9c, 10c

C. 1a alliances, b allied, c allied, d ally; 2a isolationism, b to isolate, c isolated, d isolation; 3a expansion, b to expand, c expansionists; 4a to interfere, b interference; 5a imperialism, b Imperialist, c imperial; 6a preferred, b preference; 7a containment, b contained; 8a extremely, b extreme, c extreme; 9a to cooperate, b cooperation, c cooperative; 10a communist, b communism

D. 1. major, 2. steer clear of, 3. imperialism, 4. concerned, 5. policy, 6. isolationism, 7. cooperate, 8. aid, 9. expanded, 10. extremely

E. *Possible answers:* 1. The role of the United States as a major power is a recent one. 2. Britain was ready to help enforce the Monroe Doctrine. 3. In 1819 the United States bought Florida from Spain. 4. The borders of the United States reached from the Atlantic Ocean to the Pacific Ocean. 5. The United States had the opportunity to develop an empire. 6. In 1940 the British were alone in their efforts to stop Hitler. 7. The United States and the Soviet Union were allies in World War II. 8. The Marshall Plan was one of the successes of Truman's policy. 9. Truman tried to limit the U.S. role as world policeman. 10. In the 1970s, Presidents have tried to find a position between the two extremes.

F. *Possible answers:* United, world, recent, President, to, countries, after, country, during, expanded, western, as, 1898, foreign, War, the, until, in, of, change, stop, The, to, foreign, and, tried, of, America's, between, and

Section Two

A. the, a, X, the, an, X, X, a, the, the, the, X, X, an, X, the, the, X, the, X, X, the, an, X

CHAPTER EIGHT

Section One

A. 1b, 2a, 3c, 4b, 5c, 6a, 7b, 8a, 9a, 10c

B. 1c, 2b, 3c, 4a, 5b, 6c, 7b, 8b, 9c, 10a

C. 1a character, b characteristic, c characterize, d characteristically, e characteristic; 2a materialistic, b materialism, c materials; 3a morality, b moral, c morally, d morals, e moralize; 4a abundant, b abound, c abundance, d abundantly; 5a opposed, b opposition, c opposite; 6a would face, b face, face; 7a debated, b debate, c debatable; 8a typical, b types, c typify, d typically; 9a inventor, invents, b inventiveness, c inventions, d inventive; 10a value, b valuable, c value

D. 1. face, 2. disobey, 3. unjust, 4. opposed, 5. disagreement, 6. positive, 7. immoral, 8. limited, 9. inescapable, 10. valuable.

E. the, the, X, X, X, X, X, X, the, X, X, X, the, X, X, the, the, the, X, the, the, X, the, the, a, X, the, X, X, the

F. *Possible answers*: 1. The early settlers came to the American continent for many reasons. 2. The belief in individualism has positive and negative sides. 3. Idealism and materialism are both part of the American character. 4. Thoreau opposed materialism in American life. 5. Thoreau refused to pay taxes because he opposed the Mexican-American War. 6. Thoreau was not a typical American. 7. Americans live with a compromise between idealism and materialism. 8. Americans have had to face the prospect of less abundance. 9. The debate between idealism and materialism is likely to continue in the U.S. 10. Americans can expect their government to play a larger role in their lives in the future.)

G. *Possible answers*: belief, has, sides, two, American, American, is, individual, moral, from, abundance, that, as, can, of, Fisk, the, Americans, and, with, and, individualism, most, believe, his, of

Section Two

A. See page 137.

NEWBURY HOUSE READERS

This series of books contains Readers at six proficiency levels for students of English. The vocabulary levels are:

Stage 1	300 words	Stage 4	1500 words
Stage 2	600 words	Stage 5	2000 words
Stage 3	1000 words	Stage 6	2600 words

Stage 1
Present simple
Present continuous
Past simple (1)
Future, *going to*
Modals, *can* and *must* (1)
Imperatives (1)
Questions (1, 2)
Indirect speech (1)
Determiners (1, 2)
And, but, or, because
Very

Stage 2
Future simple
Past simple (2)
Present perfect
Modals, *need, have to* (2)
Imperatives (2)
Questions (3, 4)
Conditionals (1)
Indirect speech (statements) (2)
Past participle (1)
Determiners (3)
Relatives (1)
So (=therefore)
Comparison and degree (2, 3)

Stage 3
Past continuous
Present perfect continuous
Past perfect
Modals, *may, ought/should* (3)
Passives (1)
Conditionals (2)
Reflexives (1)
Comparison and degree (4, 5)
Past participle (2)
Relative clauses (2, 3)
Indirect speech (questions, orders, requests)
-ing words (1)

Stage 4
Past perfect continuous
Future perfect
Present tenses with future reference
Modals, *might, would rather/had better* (4)
Passives (2)
Conditionals (3, 4)
Determiners (4)
Comparison and degree (6)
Relative clauses (4, 5)
Indirect speech (*whether, unless*)
-ing words (2, 3, 4)

Stage 5
Future continuous
Future perfect continuous
"Colored future"
Conditionals (5)
-ing words (5, 6, 7)
Compounds with *-ever*
Relative clauses (6, 7)
Reflexives (2)
Such after negatives
Modals, *might/would have*, etc. (5)

Stage 6
Modal verbs (6)
-ing words (8)
Impersonal forms (*It is said that . . .*)
Conditionals (6)
Relative clauses (8, 9)